CALHOUN

*John C. Calhoun Office. Clemson University Clemson, SC.
Photo Wikimedia Commons (CC0)*

CALHOUN:

A Statesman for the 21st Century

Clyde N. Wilson

SHOTWELL PUBLISHING
COLUMBIA, SOUTH CAROLINA

Calhoun: A Statesman for the 21st Century
Copyright © 2022 by Clyde N. Wilson

ALL RIGHTS RESERVED. No part of this publication may be reproduced, distributed, or transmitted in any form or by any means, including photocopying, recording, or other electronic or mechanical methods, or by any information storage and retrieval system without the prior written permission of the publisher, except in the case of very brief quotations embodied in critical reviews and certain other non-commercial uses permitted by copyright law.

Produced in the Republic of South Carolina by

SHOTWELL PUBLISHING LLC
Post Office Box 2592
Columbia, So. Carolina 29202

www.ShotwellPublishing.com

Cover Image Credit: Richard Ellis/Alamy Live News.

ISBN: 978-1-947660-69-4

First Edition

10 9 8 7 6 5 4 3 2

Contents

Preface vii

Society Before Government: Calhoun's Wisdom 1

Calhoun: American Statesman 11

John C. Calhoun and Antebellum America 25

"Free Trade: No Debt: Separation from Banks"
The Economic Platform of John C. Calhoun 37

John C. Calhoun: Anti-Imperialist
"A Wise and Masterly Inactivity" 63

Calhoun and Slavery as a "Positive Good":
What He Said 81

John C. Calhoun and Slavery as a "Positive Good":
What Calhoun *Did Not* Say 91

Cincinnatus, Call the Office! 105

Q & A on Nullification and Interposition 111

Calhoun's Carolina 117

Margaret Coit's *John C. Calhoun, American Portrait* 121

The Concurrent Majority 135

"A Senator of Rome when Rome Survived."
The Unknown Calhoun 147

About the Author 159

Cover Image

IN JUNE 2020, the officials of the City of Charleston took down a tall memorial statue of South Carolina's greatest son, an internationally recognised statesman and philosopher. The destruction of the statue took 17 hours of work with diamond-tipped saws, followed by several days reduction of the pedestal to rubble. The excuse was that Calhoun was a supporter of black slavery, a strange idea since for several centuries millions of people were supportive of such bondage.

For more than a century the monument in Marion Square was a familiar sight to Charlestonians. The Calhoun Ladies Monument Association was formed in 1854 and continued its work through War and Reconstruction. The accumulation of small donations finally allowed the erection of the statue, with a very large crowd in attendance as well as congratulatory letters from President Grover Cleveland and an address by Supreme Court Justice L.Q.C. Lamar.

The CLMA closed business in the late 19th century and donated the statue to the City of Charleston for preservation. The historic Washington Light Infantry owns the land on which the monument was located, but put up no serious objection to its destruction. Neither did the Attorney General of South Carolina, although he might have invoked a recently passed law to protect historic monuments.

Preface

FOR A LONG TIME, the careful and honest study of history as a guide to understanding human affairs was a significant part of Western discourse. Now we live in a time when a distorted, shallow, factless, one-sided, party-line history is used as a weapon to justify extortion and illegitimate power. Calhoun is a prize exhibit in the ongoing destruction of history as a high intellectual discipline.

This collection contains some of my occasional writings on Calhoun, created over a period of more than three decades. The variety of occasions results in some repetition, but I see no problem in making important and neglected points more than once in different contexts.

There is much satisfaction in having spent much of my life in almost daily communion with a great man like Calhoun. But there is also a penalty of unerasable sadness in constant reminder of how far down the American experiment in self-government has come and is going. Statesmen were rare in Calhoun's time. Today they have disappeared entirely. We know that Calhoun was a statesman because his words about government are as true and relevant today as they were in his time.

Thanks to the University Press of Virginia for permission to republish "Free Trade: No Debt: ...." from *Slavery, Secession, and Southern History*, edited by Robert Paquette; and to the University of South Carolina Press for permission to republish my Introduction to a new edition of Margaret Coit's *John C. Calhoun: American Portrait*.

I am convinced 'twas Calhoun who divined

How the great western star's last race would run.

—Allen Tate, *Fragments of a Meditation*

Society Before Government: Calhoun's Wisdom

JOHN C. CALHOUN was the last great American statesman. A statesman must be something of a prophet—one who has an historical perspective and says what he believes to be true and in the best long-range interest of the people, whether it is popular or not. A politician, which is all we have now, says and does whatever he thinks will get or keep him in power, and his historical perspective is limited to the next opinion poll or brown bag full of unmarked bills.

Calhoun's mind and his devotion to the American experiment were equal to that of the great men of the founding generation. He had an advantage over the founders in that he had 40 years of experience near the top of the federal government and thus a view of how things had worked under the Constitution. Calhoun early discerned, predicted, and warned of the tendency of the United States toward a regime of bankers and imperial overreach.

His core understanding of society and government was displayed in his *A Disquisition on Government,* which he worked on in the last months of his life and regarded as his bequest to posterity.

In the *Disquisition,* Calhoun begins, as anyone should, with human nature. Rousseau had said that men are born free and are everywhere in chains. Calhoun's first task is to free us from such nonsense. This is not because he wants to establish racial inequality or to defend slavery, but because he wants to start from sound premises. We are not born free, or equal. We are, every one of us, born as helpless, puling infants who cannot survive more than a few hours without society. However, it does not necessarily follow that we must always be in chains.

CALHOUN: A STATESMAN FOR THE 21ST CENTURY

Here is what Calhoun says about the fundamental nature of governments:

> I assume, as an incontestable fact, that man is so constituted as to be a social being. His inclinations and wants, physical and moral, irresistibly impel him to associate with his kind; and he has, accordingly, never been found, in any age or country, in any state other than the social. In no other, indeed, could he exist; and in no other—were it possible for him to exist—could he attain to a full development of his moral and intellectual faculties, or raise himself, in the scale of being, much above the level of brute creation. I next assume, also, as a fact not less incontestable, that, while man is so constituted as to make the social state necessary to his existence and the full development of his faculties, this state itself cannot exist without government. This assumption rests on universal experience. In no age or country has any society or community ever been found, whether enlightened or savage, without government of some description. But government, although intended to protect and preserve society, has itself a strong tendency to disorder and abuse of its powers, as all experience and almost every page of history testify .... The powers which it is necessary for government to possess, in order to repress violence and preserve order, cannot execute themselves. They must be administered by men in whom, like others, the individual are stronger than the social feelings. And hence, the powers vested in them to prevent injustice and oppression on the part of others, will, if left unguarded, be by them converted into instruments to oppress the rest of the community. That, by which this is prevented, by whatever name called, is what is meant by CONSTITUTION, in its most comprehensive sense, when applied to GOVERNMENT....

Constitution stands to government, as government stands to society, and, as the end for which society is ordained would be defeated without government, so that for which government is ordained would, in a great measure, be defeated without Constitution.

Think of the order of precedence Calhoun established. Society, which is ordained by God for our benefit, comes first. Government, created only by men, is something distinct that rightly exists solely for the protection of society. Further, a constitution in its true sense is that by which society limits and restrains those who are entrusted with government. It is not an open-ended charter of their powers. When a government is unrestrained, there is no constitution, by whatever name called. Today we have no constitution.

A great primary stumbling block to the building and preservation of genuine civilized communities in America is a widespread habit of thought that assumes without question that the U.S. government and the American people in their communities are all the same thing. We have to learn to distinguish between the government and our human society—society being a necessity and boon to our nature and government being only a functional arrangement. An arrangement which, according to our Declaration of Independence, may be altered or abolished when it fails to serve its purpose. For the truth of our situation today is that we are not citizens served by our government. We are taxpayers, consumers, cannon fodder. The government is not the servant of society—rather, our society is the raw material of the rulers' will to power. The U.S. government fits the founders' understanding of tyranny—a regime that tampers with, exploits, and reconstructs our communities.

When Calhoun wrote of society preceding government, he was not theorizing, unlike Rousseau and other pundits. He was recapitulating the experience of his own family and the reality of the founding of America. We need to recover some lost American history. The times have changed vastly since the founding, but perhaps a recovery of forgotten truth about American origins will inspire us to the possibilities of self-government.

BEFORE THE WAR OF CONSOLIDATION in the 1860's, Americans prided themselves that their settlements had been built by free men. The 13 colonies were not created by people who were the wards, or clients, or employees of government. Americans were people who conquered a wilderness with their own labour and capital and at the risk of their own life and limb. There was a distant Crown that theoretically was the font of land ownership. Otherwise, the colonists were men who had ventured into the wilderness by their own wills and created fresh societies while abdicating none of the rights of Englishmen. From the first they insisted on representation and making their own laws for the societies they had built.

Calhoun's own family were part of a kith of Ulstermen who came into the upcountry of South Carolina before the Revolution, when it was empty of all but hostile Indians. They were tied together not by the state but by blood, religion, necessity, and the desire to make a new life. The settlers were in fact virtually self-governing and self-reliant communities in economic, political, and military affairs. There is a very real sense in which they participated in the creation of their own government by communal acts of consent. Calhoun believed that this situation, common to Americans, had been decreed by Providence and was the source of America's prosperity and freedom. British America, he said, was settled "by hardy and enterprising immigrants. To such forebears, from the beginning thrown mostly on their own resources, Americans owed their enterprise, energy, love of liberty, and capacity for self-government."

In 1720 South Carolina became discontented when it became apparent that the Lords Proprietors intended to monopolise lands that the colonists had won by desperate efforts in war with the Indians. South Carolina had its own leaders, its own body politic, its own public opinion, its own legislature, and its own militia. Their society exercised its will, threw out the officials sent by the proprietors, and announced that South Carolina was now a regular royal colony.

FOR THE FOUNDING FATHERS, consent of the governed did not mean the political participation of the abstract individual so dear to modern democratic theory. Rather, liberty was defined by the self-determination of communities of men, preexisting historically in all their complexity and differentiation of social roles. Individual liberty meant citizenship in a free community. A community is by nature nonegalitarian and ceases to be free or even to exist when an outside power enforces an artificial equality. Liberty is not bestowed by government but is an aspect of a free society itself.

The people of South Carolina were sovereign and independent before the Declaration of Independence. Through their own governor, legislature, courts, and armed forces they were exercising every sovereign power—taxation, treaty-making, war, the execution of felons. A month before the Declaration, Colonel Moultrie and his South Carolina forces, from their palmetto log fort on Sullivan's Island, repulsed a British fleet that threatened to suppress their sovereign self-government.

This precisely describes the American War of Independence. It was not a revolution in society, but the action of the existing societies of the 13 colonies to preserve themselves against the interference of a distant government. This was the real war of the American War of independence, the preservation of living societies from the schemes of rulers. This is what the Declaration of Independence meant by "consent of the governed": The Constitution for the United States was established by free, specific acts of each sovereign people. As Madison said, the Constitution drew its authority only from the ratifications of the states. This ratification was a known historical event, and ratification could be revoked when its purpose was perverted. Unless you want to argue that the consent of the governed is something that can only be used once, like a bus ticket. This was essentially the position of Lincoln and all who have followed after him.

From the beginning, a dishonest and nationalist Revolutionary history sought to conflate American society and the machinery of the U.S. government. In the 19th century state centralization by blood and iron seemed the right and inevitable thing. Lincoln's war and Lincoln's rhetoric consummated the revolution of nationalism.

Today, the United States is a regime of Bankers, Bombers, and Busybodies. All three are deadly enemies to the preservation or building of any civilized community in North America. The desire for governmental activism always reflects a lust for power and some combination of economic profiteering and vague but strong emotions. None of these are things that nurture the higher aspirations of our human nature.

Recent history shows beyond doubt that the interest of financiers takes precedent over the welfare of the people. Military bases in over 100 countries and a prolonged war in which billions of dollars of sophisticated equipment is expended in a needless attempt to control mountain tribesmen who hate outsiders and infidels tells us about the Bombers. They reflect the triumph of nationalism over patriotism. A patriot loves his land and people, his society, because they are his. A nationalist glories in the power of his government over others. Nationalism is a defect of the spirit. It characterizes people who have no identity other than their identification with the power in the government of the nation-state. The United States is full of such people. Try starting an academic discussion of the possible benefits of secession, as I have. Your computer will be blitzed by hateful, threatening, and obscene messages from people who take any questioning of the government as sacrilege and a personal threat to themselves.

We are less aware of the depredations of the Busybodies, which often seem benevolent. Recollect George H.W Bush and Bob Dole chortling with self-satisfaction over the Americans with Disabilities Act. Who can be against helping the disabled, you ask? And I say that a government in this vast land that issues regulations covering every parking lot and building entrance, every place of refreshment and entertainment, and even every toilet has too much power. Under such a government you cannot say that you live in a free community. If the regime has the power to do whatever it likes, it has the power to do to you anything it wants. This is not a government that does what is necessary to preserve the human society that nurtures us. This is a government that assumes the power to alter us in accordance with its own notions.

There are millions of Bushes and Doles among our countrymen. They are a major American type, perhaps the predominant American type. Such people cannot distinguish human society from the U.S. government, nor can they distinguish the U.S. government from their own will. They assume it is their right to force other people .to obey their notions of doing good, and, for such people, of doing good there ain't no end. Where did George Bush get the moral authority, much less the constitutional authority, to use up American blood and treasure in the pursuit of a New World Order just because he and others think that is a good thing? His thinking was as flawed, juvenile, self-centered, and delusional as that of any infatuated dictator in history. For him our land and people were not values in themselves, just a means to carry out his delusions.

BUSH COULD GET AWAY WITH IT because he was serving the profit of powerful interests, but also because millions of Americans buy into those delusions of national grandeur and their special mission to do good. It is this kind of thinking that is the nemesis of civilization in North America. We must not heed it in rulers, and we must expunge it from ourselves. My position is at odds with European conservatism, which has made great inroads into American thought. For a European conservative, society, government, and church are or should be a whole. That is not the American tradition nor the American necessity. The tradition and necessity, for a country that has always been made up of diverse communities, is to break down and limit power—ultimately the deconstruction of the present regime.

So I come back to Calhoun. Society is given by God through human nature for our nurture. Government is needed to keep the peace, but it is also a great danger to society. We must revive the wisdom that Leviathan must be chained and disciplined to protect rather than devour us. And we must recognize that the government is never "us." The South has kept this wisdom longer than other parts of America, though it is beleaguered even there. The South, in contrast to what we know as "America," was, in the words of M.E. Bradford, a thing that was "grown, not made."

Robert Lewis Dabney, theologian and late aide to Stonewall Jackson, expressed the Southern insight in a speech to college students the year after Appomattox. The students were mostly impoverished Confederate veterans making great sacrifice to continue their education—which was typical of Southerners for the next half-century. He advises the students that they should build and secure the family and thus save the living South even under defeat and evil occupation:

> Government is not the creator but the creature of human society. The Government has no mission from God to make the community. On the contrary the community is determined by Providence, where it is happily determined for us by far other causes than the meddling of governments—by historical causes in the distant past, by vital ideas, propagated by great individual minds—especially by the church and its doctrines. The only communities which have had their characters manufactured for them by governments have had a villainously bad character, like the Chinese and the Yankees. Noble races make their governments. Ignoble ones are made by them.

Dabney was summarizing what Calhoun had said a few years earlier in his last testament to the world. And Calhoun was only putting into intellectual form what had been the doctrine of the South from the beginning. Society is natural, essential, and self-justifying, proceeding from man's God-given nature. The legitimate purpose of government is the preservation of society. Thus, the Constitution should be the instrument of society's control of government, not vice versa. This attitude can be found as far back as Bacon's Rebellion in Virginia and underlies the political thought and policy of Jefferson. A republican government was defined as a government that rested on the consent, and preserved the safety, of society. It was not created from any theoretical proposition about the Rights of Man nor any mystical emotion about the sacred nation. And, as Bradford amply showed, the American Revolution was carried out and understood as a preservation of the natural "grown" American society from the threatened dominance of a distant government that had no interest in its welfare.

Wendell Berry gives us the poet's view of the Southern tradition of society before government, saying it much better than I ever can:

> I sit in the shade of the trees of the land I was born in.
>
> As they are native I am native, and I hold to this place as carefully as they hold to it.
>
> I do not see the national flag flying from the staff of the sycamore,
>
> Or any decree of the government written on the leaves of the walnut ....

CALHOUN:
AMERICAN STATESMAN

JOHN C. CALHOUN was a major actor in the political history of 19th century America, whose dramatic career will always be of interest. However, he is equally important as a political thinker, in which he resembles the generation of the American Founding Fathers more than his own or later generations of statesmen.

Calhoun has a somewhat unique position in American history. For four decades, during a critical period of American development, he was a political figure of national power and prominence and held most of the high offices of the federal government. He was never the leader of a national party like Martin Van Buren or Henry Clay, never president like John Quincy Adams, never the beneficiary of widespread popularity like Andrew Jackson, never predominant in influence, even in the South, but he always had to be taken into account. From the beginning to the end of his career (from 1811 to 1850) he had an influence on every issue and aspect of national politics, and not merely on the questions of state rights and slavery with which his name is most commonly associated. He became, though this was not fully consummated until after his death, the political genius of the South, and thus a major protagonist in the drama of sectional conflict which is the heart and center of American history in the 19th-century.

John Caldwell Calhoun was born into a kith of hardy Ulstermen near the close of the American War of Independence (1782) in the frontier upper country of South Carolina. His family on both sides were all staunch pioneers and Patriots, leaders among their kind, who acquired as their region developed substantial but not immoderate holdings of land and slaves.

A grandmother was murdered by the Cherokees. One uncle was killed by British sabers at Cowpens, another murdered in his own yard by Tories. John's father Patrick was a frontier scout and fighter who made the arduous journey down to Charleston to vote against ratification of the new federal constitution in the State convention. Calhoun had an intimate, not theoretical, knowledge of the great achievements of American history—settling the frontier, winning independence, and establishing free institutions.

The next to youngest though ablest of four sons, his education was largely self-directed until he was well grown except for a a period at Moses Waddel's notable academy. It was good enough for him to enter the junior class at Yale University and graduate at the top in 1804. There was an early maturity and, always, a unique self-sufficiency in his intellectual life. He returned to Connecticut a few years later to study at Judge Reeve's law school—Connecticut, as is too easily forgotten, where black slaves were owned by many, including clergymen, and State rights were still preached. Where there was also a religious orthodoxy and communal social conservatism unknown in the individualistic and chivalric South.

By marriage and other connections Calhoun (and his home region) became reconciled to the polished and affluent plantation society of the lower and older part of South Carolina. For most of his forty years on the national stage he was able to speak with a kind of unanimity behind him at home that few American leaders have enjoyed. He never, contrary to what a host of superficial commentators have repeated, dictated to South Carolina; rather he led it because the state, despite occasional grumbling from ambitious and overshadowed men, recognised Calhoun as its greatest asset.

Calhoun began as, and always considered himself to be, a Jeffersonian Republican. All American questions, whatever later complications might have developed in a phenomenally expanding society, for him referred back to the primal division of Jefferson and Hamilton. However, the South Carolinians of the early Republic, among whom Calhoun grew up and fast rose to attention, were on balance slightly more commercial, cosmopolitan, martial, and amenable to vigorous government (as long as it did not serve hostile purposes) than were their great Virginia contemporaries.

Which factor goes a way to explain why he was early considered a "nationalist," relatively, among Jeffersonians; and to explain as well certain other aspects of his views.

He practiced law briefly, like Jefferson detesting it. In both cases the cast of mind was idealistic, not legalistic. Neither was willing to see the Constitution reduced to the pragmatic instrumentality of a mere lawyer's document.

After two terms in the state legislature, Calhoun was sent by his neighbors, in 1811 at the age of twenty-nine, to the House of Representatives in Washington where he enjoyed a meteoric rise to national attention. He was immediately a leader among the "War Hawks" who maneuvered a somewhat hesitant country into forceful resistance to British high-handedness. Calhoun sustained the war through every bitter setback to its glorious end. Eloquence, patriotism, steadfastness, generosity to opponents, integrity, and mastery of legislation and debate won him such compliments as "the young Hercules who carried the war on his shoulders" and "one of those master spirits who stamp their image upon the age in which they live."

From his first speech in the House, in contest with the feared John Randolph of Roanoke, Calhoun revealed himself as a statesman and not a politician, always unwilling to take short-range views or be trammeled by party considerations. From this elevated concept of his role he never deviated.

After the war he played a leading part in the perfection of the peacetime national defense establishment and in the projection of a system of internal improvements to be paid for by non-tax revenue. As chairman of a select committee on the currency he managed to get the national bank, which Madison had proposed to revive, set up on a much sounder basis than had at first been designed. In all these measures he was influenced by the near disasters of the war.

Calhoun was condemned at the time by Old Republicans as a loose constructionist, and it has been conventional to divide his career into nationalist and sectionalist phases. He could and did argue that if he had been too accepting of federal energy in his younger days, his motives had been eminently patriotic and he had been just to all sections. And that he had been in large and good company, for he had departed from Jeffersonian purity no more than had the bulk of the party and its leaders.

Further, the peacetime military establishment was a necessary and constitutional achievement. Internal improvements, as he had conceived them, were to be a truly federal program, related to defense, and not the plaything of log rolling and special interests that they actually became as the nineteenth century wore on. The moderate protective tariff which in 1816 Calhoun and other Southerners voted for, though they did not sponsor it, could be seen as temporary and as a measure of generosity toward those Northerners whose enterprise had been forced out of natural channels by the embargo and war, not intended as a permanent abrogation of free trade.

In a short view Calhoun changed his policies, as did all of the great men of the period. Taking a longer view he remained the same. His goal always was to enhance the success of the American experiment in federal republicanism by harmonizing its potentially conflicting parts. By following Calhoun from 1811 to 1850, the reader can judge for himself. I would contend that his basic vision was fully matured when he first stepped onto the national stage and did not change in its essence.

In 1817 he entered the cabinet of President Monroe as Secretary of War, chief of the largest and most far-flung of the government departments. Friends predicted that he would lose reputation in the postwar chaos of debt and disorganisation. Enemies predicted that he was too "metaphysical" to succeed as an administrator. Calhoun served to the end of the Virginia Dynasty in 1825, proved himself one of the ablest administrators the American government had yet produced, and ended, despite rocky conflicts with Congress, with his reputation enhanced. During his time in the cabinet, Calhoun and his family resided at the Georgetown estate later famous as Dumbarton Oaks and were leaders of Washington society. He was always more handsome, charming, and sociable than his textbook image has allowed.

With the disappearance of the first two-party system during the Monroe years, Calhoun, with many others, tested the presidential waters. Though he had a great deal of popularity, perhaps more in the North than in the South, he did not have enough for a clear victory and bowed out. He was still young. Instead, he was in 1824 elected vice president by a large majority, with support from the Electors of several of the four presidential candidates. At 42, he was the youngest man to have been elected president or vice president and the first who was not from Virginia, New York, or Massachusetts.

Meanwhile, the Electoral College found no majority in the presidential election, which had to be decided in the House of Representatives in favor of John Quincy Adams, amidst persistent cries of a "corrupt bargain" between Adams and Henry Clay. Calhoun separated himself from the president and from what he considered Adams's neo-Federalism, and with his followers joined the growing coalition behind General Andrew Jackson. On this ticket, which would come to be known as the Democratic party, Calhoun was reelected vice president in 1828.

The subsequent break between Jackson and Calhoun is one of the dramatic incidents of antebellum American political history. It has been told and retold by historians, usually without a very close or original look. Most of what they commonly retail is superficial if not actually wrong. In fact, it is hard to think of any part of American history that has been so persistently misrepresented. This is because many of the historians who deal with it have a vested ideological interest in a romanticized and misleading version of "Jacksonian democracy."

Calhoun hoped to see in the victory of the Jackson coalition a revival of Jeffersonian principles as they had been understood in the Monroe era—a quite reasonable hope that was shared by many others. So far as Jackson had any platform other than his popularity, that was assumed to be it.

Tensions, both personal and political, soon developed between president and vice president. Privately there were the questions of Mrs. Eaton and of the Seminole War (during which Calhoun had criticized, in confidential Cabinet discussions, the reckless actions of his then subordinate, General Jackson). Also the fact that Jackson expected the one thing that Calhoun could not give him—flattery.

More importantly, there was growing unrest in the South, and especially in Calhoun's own state, over the protective tariff. In 1828 this was raised to an unprecedented fifty percent, despite the pending retirement of the national debt, because of the backfire of an unscrupulous political maneuver carried out by Jackson's own congressional managers. Instead of the tariff being a temporary measure of aid to infant American industries forced into existence by the war, it had become a permanent system of protection for northeastern industrial interests, whose agents haunted the lobbies of Congress, the first American "lobbyists." The tariff rose ever higher, at the expense of the consumer and of the South, which lived by exporting cotton, the mainstay of the American economy, to an unprotected world market.

And instead of a Jeffersonian revival, Calhoun perceived an administration that was under the control of political managers bred in the New York school of Burr and the Clintons. Specifically of Martin Van Buren, whose services were limited to behind-the-scenes wire pulling rather than the hard road of legislative and administrative accomplishment which Calhoun had followed. Such management involved, among other things, taking a disingenuous and noncommittal middle ground on such important issues as the tariff. It also involved an unprecedented manipulation of the spoils of office. An administration which had risen to power condemning Adams on these grounds had expanded rather than retracted corruption.

Calhoun's behavior during this period, like most of his career, has been superficially characterised as the product of thwarted ambition. This impression is nothing more than demagogic slander industriously circulated by Van Burenites and other hostile politician at the time and retailed by lazy or ideologically committed historians. Had Calhoun been motivated by narrow motives of ambition, he would have gone the with the flow. He had everything to lose and nothing to gain by opposing the administration.

Instead, in 1831, Vice President Calhoun himself, not Jackson, made the whole affair of the Seminole War controversy public as a matter of honour, fully convinced that public opinion would sustain the correctness of his conduct. Into the affair of Mrs. Eaton he refused to be drawn until Eaton himself had made it public. Then it was found that the entire Cabinet, except for one, Van Buren, sided with Calhoun. It was not a matter of social snobbery, as silly historians continue to repeat, but a question of morals and the immunity of private society from political manipulation.

Further, in 1831, Vice President Calhoun made public his agreement with the doctrine called state veto, interposition, or nullification, which was rising to popularity in his own state as a remedy for the protective tariff, all other remedies having failed. In a series of public statements Calhoun took the case to the American people in sophisticated argument. His arguments remain of great interest and establish him clearly as a political thinker of permanent significance as well as an eloquent political leader. They won some adherents, but only in South Carolina was there sufficient intensity of revulsion at the tariff and sufficient political unity for a majority to adopt such a complex expedient.

As Calhoun showed, interposition—which he regarded as a last resort suspensive veto until a higher constitutional consensus of three-fourths of the states could be invoked—came naturally from the widely accepted compact fact (not theory) of the Union and was the Virginia and Kentucky doctrine of 1798-99, more seriously developed. Calhoun clearly saw it as an alternative to secession. The question he posed was: who has the final authority in Constitutional interpretation, the Supreme Court or that power which created the Constitution, the people of the States? But even in a country which still largely swore allegiance to state rights and accepted the right of secession, nullification was too impractical for wide acceptance in a system dominated by noisy party politicians.

Nevertheless, as undertaken by South Carolina in 1832-33, it could be called a limited success. Calhoun resigned as vice president during the crisis and entered the Senate with the dual purpose of defending his state and finding a solution. Congressional majorities upheld the principle of enforcement of federal laws by what Calhoun called "the Force Bill," which, however, remained unenforced. But Congress and Jackson also avoided a direct confrontation by approving a graduated reduction of the tariff down to a revenue level. It should not be forgotten that the entire South felt the tariff as a grievance, even if not willing to follow South Carolina so far, and that both sides in the controversy were led by proud, unbending Southerners.

Superficial historians, including unfortunately most of Calhoun's most recent biographers (who seem to think that historical understanding is achieved by repeating the polemics and slander arising out of one side of a controversy), have pictured to posterity a scheming and plotting Calhoun, bitter with thwarted ambitions. Or sometimes as a foolishly deluded man, half-mad with abstractions at which sensible men boggled. There is no evidence at all for either of these pictures.

A realistic understanding would suggest that Calhoun made a difficult and intelligent choice in a critical situation. He could abandon his state; or he could lead, defend, and moderate it. The choice he made was not that of a man governed by shallow personal ambition. Nor was his course a failure, as the same silly historians continue to declare.

Calhoun and his small state stood up against the federal government, overwhelming public opinion, both political parties, and the formidable popularity and temper of Andrew Jackson, went to the brink—and won concessions. Not a bad record for a politician whom a recent biographer has described as "being out of touch with reality" at this time. Not only that, but Calhoun emerged from the fray a highly respected, though certainly not a popular, public figure, which can be said of very few who went toe-to-toe with Jackson. This was because preponderant American opinion dreaded the prospect of federal coercion of a state more than it dreaded state defiance of federal law.

Calhoun was for the rest of his life a much more significant and formidable figure in American affairs than has generally been acknowledged. Although never predominant in influence, even in the South, he always had to be taken into account. He was always able to influence opinion on any issue that was up.

This unpredictable Calhoun was a thorn in the flesh of business-as-usual politicians of both parties, because he had the capacity to disrupt their convenient plans and bring up real and hard issues. For instance, in 1844 the two front-runners for presidential nominations, Henry Clay of the Whigs and Van Buren of the Democrats, mutually agreed that it was unwise for them to discuss or take position on the matter of Texas annexation, which could prove damaging to both of them. Calhoun was uninterested in presidential nominations and party welfare, but he was interested in joining Texas to the Union, and forced their hand.

There was always a considerable segment of the intelligent public, in the North as well as the South, who listened to Calhoun with attention at any juncture. The influence he exercised is all the more remarkable when it is considered that he was not widely popular, unlike Jackson or Clay; that he never had the services of a political organization of any size or effectiveness; and that many of his causes were lost. His influence was intellectual and ethical.

The ten years which followed the nullification crisis in the Senate 1833-43, are among the least noticed of Calhoun's career but perhaps the most important and the most instructive to posterity. It is during this period that the greatest number of his most profound speeches were delivered, that he brought to full development the ideas for which he is best known, that he formed with Clay and Webster the Great Triumvirate that dominated the Senate, and that he established and maintained persuasive positions on all the major issues of the day, constituting a national focal point that was often independent of both political parties.

For a while in the 1830s, loosely and for the only time, he was allied with Clay and Webster against Jackson. In the late 1830s he rejoined the Democrats and by the early 1840s was virtually their leader in the Senate. He had a large though not predominant following throughout the South. He also had substantial support and admiration, among intellectuals and at the Jeffersonian grassroots, in many parts of the North, from Boston to New York to Philadelphia to Cincinnati to Detroit.

In 1843 his friends promoted him for the Democratic presidential nomination, a campaign which he countenanced not out of ambition or hope of winning but because it gave leverage to. his principles. He did not have sufficient strength to win the nomination, but he was a major factor, among others, in at last breaking the hold of Van Buren over the party machinery and opening the way for another candidate, Polk.

In early 1844, shortly after Calhoun had retired from the Senate and withdrawn from the presidential race, the beleaguered president John Tyler, who was without the support of either party, nominated Calhoun as Secretary of State, without Calhoun's knowledge. The Union faced double crises over Oregon and Texas, the gravest juncture in foreign affairs since the War of 1812. Calhoun was unanimously confirmed by the Senate in a few hours. There was not a single dissenting vote, Democratic or Whig, Northern or Southern, though most of Tyler's nominations were routinely rejected.

Calhoun pursued the annexation of Texas to the Union, which, with the aid of Polk's victory in the election, he accomplished before he left office in 1845, without war. He also laid the groundwork for the peaceful settlement of the Oregon issue with Great Britain. This was eventually concluded on the basis Calhoun had outlined, but not before two years of unproductive bluster and dangerous brinksmanship on the part of the succeeding administration.

It was generally expected that Polk would ask Calhoun to remain as Secretary of State, because of his services to the party and country and to finish the matters he had in hand. But where Calhoun sat was the head of the table, and Polk offered him instead the ambassadorship to Great Britain, which he knew Calhoun would refuse.

So Calhoun retired to Fort Hill, the plantation in the lovely foothills in the western corner of South Carolina that he had begun developing when he was vice president. There he had raised a large family of children, was a pillar of the neighborhood, and was happily occupied, whenever possible, as a farmer. It was only a middling plantation by South Carolina standards, but a diversified and self-sufficient one.

Nine months later Calhoun returned reluctantly to the Senate to remain for over four years and die at his post in 1850. These last years provide another chapter of his career and his political thought. He devoted himself to two concerns and became for the fast time a pessimist and a stern critic of the course that American society was taking.

He provided a restraining influence on jingoism and imperialism, which were being promoted enthusiastically by many of the politicians later to be celebrated by historians as paragons of democracy and the common man. In the case of the Mexican War, he risked his standing in the South to pursue an independent policy. While supporting the forces, he strove for limited war aims, tried to dampen thoughtless expansionism, warned that territorial acquisitions would create insoluble problems between the North and the South, and prophesied that the way the war had been initiated had created perilous precedents of presidential usurpation.

The second concern of his last years was the intransigent sectional conflict over slavery. As a member of the cabinet during the Missouri controversy, in the early 1820s, he had supported the Compromise. He had also sought to defuse the unrest of his fellow Southerners, at the same time quietly warning his Northern friends that here was the only issue that could break the Union.

Not until the mid-1830s, when antislavery became abolitionism and took on a new and militant cast, impatient and with hatred for everything Southern, did Calhoun draw a line in the dust. This was deplored by the major political leaders of both parties, North and South. Most of them were either indifferent to slavery or as committed to its defense as was Calhoun, but they apparently hoped that ignoring the issue and keeping it as much as possible out of attention would allow them to muddle through.

Once he had sensed the intransigence of the new movement, Calhoun refused to take a short-tern view or to countenance the expectation of an easy answer. By the time of the Wilmot Proviso of 1846, he had become convinced that the South had to achieve internal unity, to meet all attacks at the threshold, and to insist on a fair share of the western territories, or it faced subjugation or extinction.

It should be remembered that in his lifetime Calhoun never dominated the South, though he led a part of it. Most Southerners, like most people most of the time, preferred to live in the short-run, ignore distant threats, and hope for the best. Calhoun's efforts were directed primarily at unifying the South, not at fighting the North. Unified, the South would be strong enough to defend itself and put off the crisis that would otherwise inevitably destroy the Union. But it was not until after his death, when the intransigence of sectional struggle had become apparent to all, that the Southern majority found itself where Calhoun had been all along. For better or worse, history provides few such examples of one thinker having led a people so dramatically, after his death. Calhoun had performed for the South, and for America, the true and essential service of a statesman: he had defined for them their alternatives.

The alternatives that Calhoun posed for Americans in regard to the slavery question were stark and unpalatable but true. So much so that he appears at the end of his life, in the midst of the negotiations from which issued the doomed Compromise of 1850, as a sad prophet of civil war. Either the majority must will itself to abide by the Constitution and keep hands off the minority in the matter that was most unique and problematic to itself—or bloodshed, dissolution of the Union, and the loss of mankind's best hope would follow.

Writers of various stamp have in the twentieth century analyzed and praised Calhoun as a valuable commentator and even as a prophet in regard to democratic pluralism, class conflict, modern interest group politics, international organizations, and even affirmative action. While all of these approaches have some validity, each of them, it seems to me, is misleading taken alone.

To political scientists Calhoun is known for the concurrent majority, not always clearly defined or understood, and to historians as the defender of state rights and black slavery. There remains much to be said about various unexplored aspects of his political thought, but the most pressing need is to see its range and wholeness.

It is of limited usefulness to discuss Calhoun's thought in terms of the influences upon him, in the manner of literal-minded scholars: "Calhoun got this from Aristotle" or "Calhoun revised Madison's faction theory here." This is a sophomoric way of approaching the subject. Calhoun was an original thinker; that is, he made use of his intellectual heritage in his own way, for his own purposes.

Unlike Daniel Webster or Thomas Hart Benton or Charles Sumner, he does not stud his speeches with bookish allusions to display his learning. His library was dispersed at the death of his eldest son and cannot be recovered. This, together with the paucity of direct allusions to other thinkers, limits what we can know about influences. We do know that he was well educated in the classics and modem history. He was also interested in political science, theology, economics, the applied sciences, and other subjects, and studied hard and purposefully all his life.

However, except in the treatise *A Disquisition on Government*, finished late and posthumously published, he does not present himself as a political philosopher. He is a public man engaged in addressing his fellow legislators and citizens—a rhetorician in the great Anglo-Saxon tradition of parliamentary deliberation which reached its height in the late eighteenth and early nineteenth centuries.

He is always dealing with a real and known audience and with a subject requiring decision. Even so, he is a political thinker because his arguments are always cast in philosophical terms, they aim at the true and the right and at the long-term best interests of the commonwealth. Calhoun always sought to persuade, never merely to posture or impress. He was never superficial, never condescended to or tricked his audience. As one biographer has said, "he dignified every question he embraced."

In his own time, Calhoun was an unfashionable orator, without the ornamentation and theatrical flourishes that were typical of the other great speakers of the day. And the most common criticism of his writings, by pragmatic-minded politicians and journalists, was that they were too philosophical for the commonsense American world. It is just these two qualities of simplicity and higher generalization that make his words all the more durable—still alive in another age when those of his critics are dead on the page.

Your ordinary run-of-the mill historian will tell you that John C. Calhoun, having defended the bad and lost causes of state rights and slavery, deserves to rest forever in the dustbin of history. Nothing could be further from the truth. No American public figure after the generation of the Founding Fathers has more to say to later times than Calhoun. Calhoun must be studied and understood in the realm of prophecy.

John C. Calhoun

and Antebellum America

FOR ONE WHO SPENDS as much time as I have with John C. Calhoun and his literary remains, is indeed a challenge to gain enough perspective to focus on what is most useful to convey to you in a few minutes.

Everyone who deals with Calhoun either admires him or hates him, and I may as well say up front that I find much to admire in this great villain of American history. Calhoun was a major fixture in the American landscape for forty years—from 1811, when, after his first speech in the House of Representatives, he was called by Thomas Ritchie in the Richmond *Enquirer* "one of those master-spirits, who stamp their names upon the age in which they live," until his death in 1850.

Though during this period Calhoun held various federal offices—representative from South Carolina, secretary of war, vice president, secretary of state, and senator from South Carolina—and was at least twice a moderately serious candidate for a presidential nomination, he was never a party leader or a figure of mass popularity like Andrew Jackson or Henry Clay. He was almost always outside the two-party system or else at odds with the leadership of his party. He had many admirers, North and South, however, and he was always important—what he had to say commanded public attention and influenced public opinion on every question of the middle period of American history.

His importance exceeds the sum total of the offices he held and his direct political power. Calhoun, with a few followers, sometimes held a balance of power between the parties in Congress, but, more importantly, he exercised the power of ideas over his time. One simply cannot understand American history between Jefferson and the Civil War without taking Calhoun into account.

The intense and emaciated Calhoun that stares out at us from the Matthew Brady daguerreotype, taken in the last few years of his life, conveys a certain image that goes along with the oft-quoted description of Calhoun by an Englishwoman, Harriett Martineau: "A cast-iron man, who looks as though he had never been born and never can be extinguished."

In fact, the Brady likeness was taken when Calhoun was old and sick, and Harriett Martineau met him only briefly. Throughout most of his career and for most of those with whom he came in contact Calhoun was considered to be a handsome, charming, and even dazzling individual; a view which is supported by his portraits in youth and middle age. His influence would not have been so great otherwise, certainly. While Calhoun is most often thought of as theoretical and rather fanatical, I will argue to the contrary: he was the least narrow and legalistic, the most philosophical and far-seeing of the statesmen of his generation.

It is impossible in the time we have together for me to go into much depth about Calhoun and about the issues and policies of what is to me the exciting and vital middle period of American history. I will be content if I am able to leave you with a few impressions that will revise the "cast-iron man" image of the textbooks and point direction to some of the complexities of this formative era in the American experience that are not always taken account of adequately.

Let me touch on just a few points that illuminate Calhoun personally, before I go to the main course of my presentation—the main course being a look at Calhoun's role in relation to some of the issues of the 1830s and 1840s that are less known than his career as a young War Hawk, than nullification, or than his last years of anti-abolitionism, and yet are important parts of Calhoun's impact on his times.

There was a Calhoun who was the indulgent father of seven children. A Calhoun who could charm in private conversation all comers—male and female, young and old, rich and plain, American and foreign. There was a Calhoun who had such a characteristically American enthusiasm for material progress that in his fifties he spent nine days on horseback clambering over the most rugged part of the Appalachians to settle for himself a disagreement about the best route for a railroad, and who invested his spare capital in a Georgia gold mine whose mechanical and chemical operations fascinated him. Then there was Calhoun the farmer, who regretted every moment spent away from home and would not travel on the political circuit, refusing countless invitations to dinners in his honor in every part of the United States.

None of these Calhouns can be any more than hinted at by way of contrast to the "cast-iron man" image. Then there was Calhoun the political thinker who has remained of perennial or at least of recurrent interest to observers of diverse time, climes, and viewpoints. More so than any of his contemporaries or later actors in American public life he remains of interest for his intellectual legacy. And to a degree that ranks him with the generation of Founding Fathers among Americans in his combination of thought with public life. Indeed, one scholar, though not an admirer, has entitled a recent article: "John C. Calhoun: Last of the Founding Fathers." *The Cambridge History of American Literature* of the early twentieth century observed of Calhoun's oratory, correctly: "Even when discussing subjects of bygone interest he commonly struck at fundamentals and at principles with such force and precision that many of his words still have vitality." Attention from students of political thought and intellectual history—as opposed to political historians—has been recurrent and for the most part favorable.

Just to cite the literature that appeared within a few years of 1950 will indicate the range of Calhoun interests. There appeared Charles Wiltse's three-volume scholarly biography and Margaret Coit's one-volume popular biography—both models of their kind. Also August O. Spain's *The Political Theory of John C. Calhoun* and Richard Current's study. Calhoun is the hero of *The American Heresy* by the British historian Christopher Hollis and of *Freedom and Federalism* by the American commentator Felix Morley. Among the articles appearing at the time: Richard Hofstadter's famous and misleading "John C. Calhoun: Marx of the Master Class"; Russell Kirk's chapter on "Calhoun and Minorities" in *The Conservative Mind*; Peter Drucker's "A Key to American Politics: Calhoun's Pluralism"; and Ralph Lerner's "Calhoun's New Science of Politics." This is only to scratch the surface.

And I may say that the 1980s witnessed a similar spate of literature including three biographies and studies in England, Italy, and Japan. Examples of recent interest: Vukan Kuic's "John C. Calhoun's Theory of the Concurrent Majority," widely circulated in the *American Bar Association Journal*; Ronnie W. Faulkner's "Taking John C. Calhoun to the UN"; and the black scholar Hanes Walton, who in *The Political Philosophy of Martin Luther-King* has related Calhoun's ideas to recent questions of minority rights.

Since our subject is Calhoun and antebellum America, I must resist the temptation to expand on these matters. I would like instead to concentrate on certain aspects of Calhoun's role in antebellum American politics as a legislator and as an intellectual balance of power between the Whigs and the Democrats. In doing so, I shall avoid the best-known issues of nullification, tariff, and slavery. I shall concentrate on a period from the late 1830s to the middle 1840s, between the nullification episode and the Wilmot Proviso, and on three issues—banking and currency, the public lands, and the Oregon question.

During this period Calhoun shows to best advantage. He was a freelance statesman who refused to be tied closely to either party and who took far-sighted views on the issues of the day. He was widely admired by many of the independent-minded, in the North as well as the South. Curiously, though he had considerable support in the South, he never, contrary to later impressions, enjoyed a dominant role in southern politics during his lifetime.

The question of banking and currency in the Jacksonian period was extremely vital and extremely complicated. Like most economic issues it involved symbols and values as well as material interests. American historians have not done justice to this question, have not made the issues clear regarding the controversies over the Bank of the United States, the Independent Treasury, and the currency. Between 1834 and 1843 Calhoun devoted more attention in the Senate to the financial question than to any other. In a series of magnificent speeches he clarified the issues as well as they ever have been and staked out a position independent of both parties.

He did it so ably that Bray Hammond, the leading historian of American banking, has written that Calhoun was the only statesman of the time to really understand the question. Calhoun condemned both the Democrats and Whigs for a failure to understand and deal honestly with the real issues and characterized the struggle between the parties over the Bank as largely meaningless. He accurately predicted the panic that occurred in 1837 and made specific, constructive proposals in both monetary and fiscal policy.

Calhoun had played a role in the charter of the second Bank of the United States in 1816. The charter had been proposed by President Madison and his Treasury Department, but Calhoun had gotten it amended in the House to provide some safeguards for the public. President Andrew Jackson vetoed the renewal of the Bank's twenty-year charter, sponsored by Henry Clay, and then withdrew the government deposits from their legal resting place in the Bank and put them into institutions picked by his own administration. This inaugurated a struggle that did not end till the Civil War.

In the Senate, Calhoun analyzed with merciless logic the illegality and sophistry of Jackson's proceedings and supported Clay's resolutions of censure. However, he took pains to distinguish his position from that of the Whigs. He was an opponent of presidential usurpation but no longer an advocate of the Bank of the United States. The smoke and din of party warfare had obscured the real issue, which was control of the currency. This properly and constitutionally belonged to the Congress and could not be delegated away to the executive branch or to any semi-private bank or set of banks. Later in the debate he went beyond the question of the power and responsibility to provide the country with "a uniform, stable, and safe currency"—which both parties were shirking—and spoke also of the need "to guard against dangerous control of one class over another."

He agreed with the Whigs that the Bank had provided a stable currency, but he regarded the previous arrangement as giving too much public power not only to that bank but to the whole banking system. He agreed with the Democrats that the Bank had dangerous power. But there must be a gradual and responsible change to another system, not merely the substitution of a host of "pet banks" for the Bank of the United States. He pointed out that whether there was a national bank or not, the government was tied to the whole banking system by the fact that it received bank notes in its collections—something which had been quietly and deliberately adopted as a practice by Alexander Hamilton and continued ever since. The Congress was in effect delegating its power over the currency and furthermore lending its own credit to the power and profit of private institutions. This, like the tariff, was simply means of profiting certain interests, with no service or risk to themselves, at the expense of the community.

After the removal of the deposits and the institution of the "pet bank" system by Jackson, Calhoun introduced and played the leading role in getting passed the Deposit Act of 1836, which regulated the banks in which the government funds were deposited, forced the banks to pay for the privilege of holding government funds, and prevented the fraud, inflation, and default that had taken place. In addition, the act provided for surplus revenue to be distributed to the states rather than held inactive for the use of the banks. The Jacksonians, calling themselves friends of the people, had shown no hesitancy in distributing the public funds among the favored banks and the public lands among the favored speculators. Why were they so averse to a return of the over-collected tax revenue back to the states? "Was it to prevent the people from being corrupted? Were the people alone capable of being corrupted? Were the government and banks all pure, while the people alone were corrupt and corruptible?"

In September 1837 Calhoun made a great speech supporting President Van Buren's first hints about the establishment of an Independent Treasury, which it could be said that Calhoun had inspired. He put aside his opposition to Van Buren for the national crisis. It was time that Congress undertook its responsibility for a stable currency and separated the government from private privilege and profit. To the bill to set up the subtreasury he introduced an amendment to gradually eliminate the government's receiving of bank notes, which in effect had made private bank notes the national currency. He desired, he said, to separate the government and the banks. The next step would be a reliable currency provided by the government itself. His plan was adopted and passed the Senate but did not come to vote in the House at that session.

The currency and banking issue see-sawed back and forth throughout the nineteenth century. The subtreasury, along the lines Calhoun had proposed, was adopted in 1846 but thrown out in favor of a national banking system in 1861. It is not too much perhaps to suggest that if his measures had been carried out much of the economic stress and upheaval and political turmoil over the currency that marked the later nineteenth century could have been avoided.

His interest in banking and currency was related to deep study of other economic issues—the tariff, the revenues and expenditures of the government, and the national debt. He opposed the frequent resorts of the government to raising loans, which he characterized as simply the government borrowing from others on its own credit and profiting private interests who risked nothing. In economic matters Calhoun was a liberal in all the best senses of that word. The eloquence with which he outlined the moral degradation and undermining of republican virtue and patriotism that resulted from the legislative manipulations of various interests is still moving.

A related issue on which Calhoun made far-seeing though unsuccessful legislative efforts was the public lands. These were the government's chief source of revenue after the tariff. Having been given up generously by the old states, Calhoun felt, the public lands were the chief endowment of the Union and of posterity. In 1837

Calhoun first proposed (and reintroduced many times later) his bill to cede the public lands which remained unsold after a time on the market to the western "new" states in which they were situated. This would free the federal government from a major source of corruption and free the newer states from vassalage. Further, it would be a gesture of generosity from the East to the West that would cement the bonds of Union. Some of the revenue would still go to the government and the lands would still get into the hands of settlers.

Both the Jacksonians and the Whigs preferred instead to distribute revenue from the public lands to all the states, which was politically attractive but to Calhoun immoral. Such distribution would be a squandering of the endowment of the Union and a breach of faith with the old states that had given up their land claims to provide the government with revenue; it would provide an excuse for keeping up the tariff to high levels; continue all the expense and corruption attendant upon the federal administration of the lands; and encourage the states to irresponsible debt in the expectation of surplus revenue.

When the distribution was passed in 1841, Calhoun managed to get an amendment providing that the distribution would be suspended if the tariff went above a certain level. It was so suspended in a brief time and the whole project proved a disaster, throwing many states into disgraceful default, as Calhoun had predicted. By Calhoun's plan the states would have had a secure endowment which they could have used as they wished. This would have put the internal improvements power directly into the hands of the states and eliminated another troublesome and corrupting national issue. This was clearly realized by Abraham Lincoln, at that time a member of the Illinois legislature, who wrote his congressman in enthusiastic support of Calhoun's plan. (Lincoln's sponsorship of an ambitious but failed internal improvements program resulted in bankruptcy of the Illinois government.)

It is possible to argue that Calhoun's proposal was superior both to the disastrous distribution adopted by both Whigs and Democrats and to the Republican's Homestead Act which led to disastrous over-production on the plains and to the abuses of vast giveaways to railroads which followed the Civil War. Again, Calhoun took a statesmanlike and far-seeing position, though opposed by the more "practical" politicians of both parties.

Professor Merrill D. Peterson has observed quite rightly: "Calhoun's whole tendency...was to approach issues theoretically rather that practically and to seek resolution the hard way, on principles, rather than by balancing interests and accommodation to circumstances." This is a true and insightful observation to which I would add three interpretive comments.

1.) This tendency did not prevent Calhoun as a legislator from being flexible and compromising as to circumstances, details, and timing as long as principles were kept in view. In both the long struggles, over banking and the public lands, he showed a good deal of flexibility and a willingness to take account of all interests and proceed gradually and justly.

2.) While many thought of Calhoun as "impractical," this was indeed the source of such political strength, popularity, and influence as he had. It was widely recognized and almost as widely admired that Calhoun would stake out principled positions and adhere to them. The public knew that his stands were not merely tactics, as in the case of many other politicians, and for this reason Calhoun had more influence over the debate than his numerical following justified.

3.) If not practical, Calhoun's views always entailed a high and strenuous view of democracy and self-government. He actually believed that once enlightened the people would do what was right, even at a sacrifice. Calhoun regarded politics not as the dividing up of the pie among various interests but as a high and principled activity designed to nourish the long-range health of a constitutional federal republic. In this he resembles the Founding Fathers, who, after all, very impractically made a revolution over a trifling tax on tea because of the principle involved. This was, in the final analysis, Calhoun's position on slavery. Calhoun was not alone in defending slavery—if he had been some of the unpopularity he has suffered would be justified. Many American statesmen defended slavery. But Calhoun insisted, as Lincoln did later in a different way, that the issue had to be faced squarely and settled permanently rather than papered over with expedient compromises that would not last.

The last issue I wish to discuss is Calhoun's role in the settlement of the Oregon controversy with Great Britain, while he was senator and secretary of state in the mid-1840s. There were significant American elements that either through belligerence or short-sightedness were prepared to press a conflict to the point of war for the whole of the Oregon territory, though Britain was ready for a peaceful compromise. This was the attitude of the Democratic party and of President Polk when he took office, following Calhoun's period as secretary of state. Whatever else may be said about Calhoun's year as secretary of state, and it is perhaps the most criticized period of his career, he showed the highest statesmanship in the Oregon controversy.

The territory had long been jointly and peacefully occupied. As early as 1842 there were efforts in Congress to terminate joint occupancy and authorize occupation in force by Americans, which would have been a clear violation of treaty. In a great speech in early 1843, Calhoun fully laid out to the Senate both the dishonour and unwisdom of such a proceeding. If Americans would only wait, he said, and trust in the dynamism of themselves and their democratic institutions, they would win all to which they had a just claim without war. If they forced the conflict they would be in the wrong and would be foolishly bringing about a situation of which no man could predict the outcome.

This was a masterful piece of diplomatic, military, historical, and moral reasoning, which won the acclaim of all sensible Americans of both parties at the time. Calhoun received many letters of congratulation and appreciation from northerners. In that speech he presented the basis which he acted upon not long after as secretary of state, taking the negotiations over Oregon as far as was possible toward a peaceful settlement in the short time he had and during an election in which Oregon was a hot issue.

The last chapter of this has to do with his relations wit President Polk after Calhoun returned to the Senate. If one reads Polk's famous diary closely, one will see that Calhoun, in his conversations with the president, was trying with great tact, skill, and modesty to persuade Polk into a sensible position—to reopen negotiations and settle at the Forty-ninth Parallel for a division of territory. I ask anyone who doubts this to look at Polk's diary entries for February 25, 1846, and March 30, 1846, Polk recorded Calhoun's suggestions, the import of which he did not realize, and which he resisted strenuously. But in the end, within two months in fact, Polk was forced to do everything that Calhoun had suggested: accepting the dividing line, bypassing certain questions of etiquette to re-open negotiations, consulting the Senate in advance, and all in contradiction to his own platform and previous position. Needless to say, this did not endear Calhoun to the President.

When Calhoun tried to apply the same tactful persuasion in regard to Mexico, in order to achieve American objectives while avoiding war, Polk rebelled even as his party began to fall apart. He began to complain to his diary that Calhoun was the most dangerous man in the Congress and was attempting to destroy Polk to serve his own consuming ambition for the presidency.

Politicians who found themselves blocked or shown up by Calhoun's foresight always reverted to the explanation that his appeals to principle were really only mischievous efforts to undermine party unity and practical politics for his own benefit. Perhaps they found it hard to believe that a public man could act from other motives. The contemporary portrayal of Calhoun as consumed by ambition, made by such lesser figures as Polk and Thomas Hart Benton, has been more often than not adopted by historians. This despite the self-evident fact that over and over again in his life Calhoun sacrificed a growing popularity to take a position that he felt was in the long run correct though unpopular.

In relation to this tale of Calhoun's consuming and warping ambition for the presidency, let me conclude with. a contrasting statement by Robert M. T. Hunter of Virginia, for years one of Calhoun's closest associates and allies. He wrote a fragmentary memoir of Calhoun, which has rested for many years nearly unnoticed in the Virginia State Library:

Whether Mr, Calhoun ever regarded himself as having any real chance for the presidency, I did not then & do not now know. But then and now I have supposed that he did not really believe that he had any such chance. But Mr. Calhoun had a theory that no man could perform a first rate part in Federal politics or in the arena of Washington if no one supposed that he was available then or could be so hereafter as a candidate for the presidency. He would therefore exert himself to keep whatever apparent claims or chances he might have for the presidency whether he really hoped for it or not. To keep up and increase if possible his power of usefulness was always a first rate object with him which in his eyes would have justified any exertion.

I submit that Calhoun was not a serious aspirant for the presidency after 1833 and was not consumed, as so many historians have repeated, with ambition for that office. He was too perceptive to believe that he had any chance after nullification. Rather, he was pursuing a very skillful policy of balance of power between parties, seeking to be the flywheel that regulated the running of the machinery of the Union and kept it from flying apart from its own energy. The flywheel in fact was a favorite image which he used often in speeches. For some years in the vital middle period of American history he carried out this role successfully in a way that has no precedents or successors in American history.

Presented at the David A Sayre History Symposium,
Sayre School, Lexington, Kentucky, 1986

"Free Trade: No Debt: Separation from Banks" The Economic Platform of John C. Calhoun

> The conservatives of the Old South believed that the preservation of a society's spiritual and moral values depends to a significant extent upon the nature and form of its property.
>
> —Eugene D. Genovese,
> *The Southern Tradition: The Achievements and Limitations of an American Conservatism* (1994)

IT IS CURIOUS how little attention has been paid to John C. Calhoun's economics. Between the resolution of the nullification conflict (1833) and the Wilmot Proviso (1846)—fully a third of his career—the greater part of his public life was directed toward matters of economics. He paid some attention in this period to foreign affairs and to threshold defenses against the as-yet-weak threat of abolitionism, but Calhoun devoted more study and more major speeches to economic questions than all other subjects put together.

In so doing he developed comprehensive programs, distinct from those of *both* the Whigs and the Democrats, in regard to the tariff, government finance, the public lands, internal improvements, and especially currency and banking—all the vexed issues of the "Jacksonian" era. His program won adherents and admirers from both parties and was regarded by many thoughtful Americans, as much or more in the North as the South, as exemplary of true republican statesmanship.

The issues were all interrelated, of course, and all integral to the great theme of the period as Calhoun saw it, the maintenance of prosperity and harmony in the wake of a vast expansion and development of the Union. Many at the time thought that Calhoun platform came closer to being principled and reasoned than did the often expedient positions of the two parties. In a speech of 1842 Calhoun summarized his position: "Free Trade: Low Duties: No Debt: Separation from Banks: Economy: Retrenchment: and Strict Adherence to the Constitution." This was used by his supporters as a slogan in his campaign for the 1844 Democratic presidential nomination and was emblazoned on the front page of the Washington *Spectator,* the campaign newspaper.

The neglect of Calhoun's economics is even more surprising when one remembers that as long ago as 1957, Bray Hammond, generally considered the best historian of banking, praised Calhoun's understanding as superior to that of the other statesmen of the time.[1] Of Calhoun's numerous biographies and book-length commentaries, only one has given any significant attention to his banking and currency proposals—the central issue of the period. That was the 1903 work by Gustavus M. Pinckney, a South Carolina lawyer and amateur scholar.[2] Some authors—Coit, Wiltse, Styron, Marmor[3]—have paid attention to Calhoun's thought in the broad sense of a philosophic defense of an agrarian economy and society, but even these have not consistently and thoroughly examined how his principles were formulated and defended in the legislative battles of the time, though there have been a few specialized articles on some aspects.[4]

---

1 Bray Hammond, *Banks and Politics in America: From the Revolution to the Civil War* (Princeton, N.J., 1957), 37, 111, 234-37, 367-68, 427-29, 609.

2 Gustavus M. Pinckney, *Life of John C. Calhoun: Being a View of the Principal Events of His Career and an Account of His Contributions to Economic and Political Science* (Charleston, S.C., 1903).

3 Margaret L. Coit, *John C. Calhoun: American Portrait* (Boston, 1950); Charles M. Wiltse, *John C. Calhoun,* 3 vols. (Indianapolis, 1944-51); Arthur M. Styron, *The Cast-Iron Man: John C. Calhoun and American Democracy* (New York, 1935); Theodore R. Marmor, *The Career of John C. Calhoun: Politician, Social Critic, Political Philosopher* (New York, 1988).

4 Noteworthy are Magdalen Eichert, "John C. Calhoun's Land Policy of Cession," *South Carolina Historical Magazine* 55 (Oct. 1954), 198 209, and John L. Larson, "'Bind

In fact, one may say that "Jacksonian" historians as a group have done an abysmal job of explaining the economic issues of the period. There are many reasons for this, in addition to the complexity of the subject. For a long time, Federalist/Republican historiography reigned supreme, dismissing southern opposition to the northern version of economic nationalism as simply stupid and evil, just as Calhoun's opponents sometimes did in his day.

Later, an influential school of historians tended to promote a romanticized version of "Jacksonian democracy," portending the New Deal. Historians such as Bowers, Schlesinger, Remini, and Niven have adopted the negative and minimizing view of Calhoun held by the Free-Soil wing (a minority) of the Democratic party. Remini, for instance, pictured Calhoun as grinding his teeth over his "own foolish mistakes," and Niven portrays him as "out of touch with reality."[5] Neither has paid any attention to his bills or speeches, which reveal him to be not the Marx of the Master Class, as Richard Hofstadter wrote, but in many ways a better "Jacksonian" than his principal Democratic opponents— whose adherence to free trade or opposition to the national bank were sometimes compromised by political expediency and disguised profiteering as well as inconsistencies that Calhoun never exhibited. (Democratic senators from New York, Pennsylvania, and lower New England, pledged to a free trade platform, always voted to raise tariffs, as Calhoun often pointed out.)

By the time serious historians had undermined the romantic myth of anti-business Jacksonians, attention had shifted massively to slavery, in the light of American preoccupation with racial issues, leaving no market for a close examination of Calhoun as economist.

---

the Republic Together': The National Union and the Struggle for a System of Internal Improvements," *Journal of American History* 74 (Sept. 1987): 363-87.

5 Robert V. Remini, *Martin Van Buren and the Making of the Democratic Party* (New York, 1951), 184; John Niven, *John C. Calhoun and the Price of Union: A Biography* (Baton Rouge, La., 1988), 178-99. See also Claude G. Bowers, *Party Battles of the Jackson Period* (1922), and Arthur M. Schlesinger Jr., *The Age of Jackson* (1945).

Of course, economics is a very imperfect "science." As a correspondent once observed to Calhoun, in economics "sequences are not always consequences." Multiple variables are always at work, and there are always political and ideological incentives to make claims for sequences as consequences of particular ideas, policies, or conditions, or of the supposed virtues of particular politicians. And it is as often in the interest of politicians to obfuscate as to clarify—as Calhoun frequently pointed out in debate.

These difficulties perhaps explain why historians in general have tended to portray the Jacksonian controversy over banking and currency in terms of stale political polemics rather than pursue its complexities to the bottom. There have been a number of original contributions, such as Hammond's emphasis on the influence of expansive New York banking interests behind the allegedly "hard-money" Jacksonian attack on the second Bank of the United States and Peter Temin's discovery of the critical impact of Mexican silver on the American currency situation.[6] But general accounts of the era have shown little impact of these or other complicating insights.

I cannot presume here to fully explicate the tortured issue of banking and currency and the other economic questions that Calhoun addressed. However, they can be somewhat illuminated by close attention to Calhoun's ideas and positions because Calhoun, always casting himself in the role of high statesman, was engaged in clarifying the issues for his own time, in providing alternatives to party gimmicks, and in clearing away common political distortions and public misunderstandings that stood in the way, in his view, of truth and the harmonious progress of the Union. Whatever else may be said of Calhoun, his arguments were never superficial or expedient.

Thus an examination of Calhoun's economic arguments and legislation should enrich our understanding of the "Jackson" period and of the mind of the Old South. And a proper understanding of these matters will be seen to support nicely in nearly every aspect

---

6   Peter Temin, *The Jacksonian Economy* (New York, 1969).

the description of the worldview of the planter class that has been developed by Eugene Genovese in recent books—its interest in material progress, but a progress morally centered and preservative.

One of the great paradoxes of American history is that the conservative South has often been the fount and mainstay of "liberal" and "democratic" movements. Without the South there would have been no Jeffersonian democracy and no Jacksonian democracy in the forms that occurred (not to mention later populist uprisings)—as the most casual glance at voting statistics will prove. The conservative regime of the South has often been the chief obstacle to the bourgeois conservatism of the business classes. The latter needed a strong national government for protected markets, credit expansion, infrastructure expenditures, and much else. This has led to a permanent confounding in American discourse (as Russell Kirk has pointed out) of the "conservative tendency" with the often incompatible "acquisitive instinct."[7]

This mistake the South never made. The South's organic conservatism was' complete, in a sense, at the plantation level, and no activist government was needed. Eugene Genovese has explicated with great depth and subtlety the organic conservatism that reached its heights in the South in the 1850s after Calhoun's death. One can see an early sign of this in Calhoun when he told the Senate in 1838:

> The Southern States are an aggregate, in fact, of communities, not of individuals. Every plantation is a little community, with the master at its head, who concentrates in himself the united interests of capital and labor, of which he is the common representative. These small communities aggregated make the state, in all whose action, labor, and capital is equally represented and perfectly harmonized. Hence the harmony, the union, and stability of that section, which is rarely disturbed except through the action of this Government. The blessing of this state of things

---

7   Russell Kirk, *The Conservative Mind: From Burke to Eliot,* 4th ed. (New York, 1968), 80.

extends beyond the limits of the South. It makes that section the balance of the system; the great conservative power, which prevents other portions, less fortunately constituted, from rushing into conflict.[8]

In his economic and constitutional views Calhoun was free to remain essentially an eighteenth-century Jeffersonian republican. Indeed Calhoun's mature program coincides almost exactly with the views of the Old Republicans and the later Jefferson, as expressed in Jefferson's elaboration of his famous avowal that the "earth belongs in usufruct to the living."[9] Jefferson's statement implied the "liberal" economic freedom of the current generation, but also a "conservative" moral responsibility to future generations in regard to public debt.

If Calhoun's goal was the defense of an organic society, that did not imply a reactionary state on the European model or a mercantilist state on the British and northern pattern. In fact, a loose republican confederation with a limited central power was the best possible government for an organic society. The South required only free markets and a purely local labor discipline.

Thus Calhoun's political economy expressed economic liberalism and a society of independent though morally responsible freeholders—an ideal that had powerful appeal to many Americans beyond the South. This ideal is why Calhoun was the preferred national leader

---

8   Remarks, 10 Jan. 1838, *The Papers of John C. Calhoun* (Columbia, S.C., 1959-), 14:84-85.

9   Jefferson's ideas in regard to public debt and currency coincide nearly exactly in spirit and specifics with those elaborated by Calhoun. See especially his letters to John Wayles Eppes, 24 June 1813, and to Samuel Kercheval, 12 July 1816, *The Works of Thomas Jefferson,* ed. Paul Leicester Ford, 12 vols. (New York, 1905), 11:297-306, 12:3-15. See also Carey M. Roberts, "The Great Compact, Dual Federalism, and Nullification: The Conservatism of Patrick Henry, John Randolph, Nathaniel Macon, and John C. Calhoun" (M.A. thesis, University of South Carolina, 1995). Schlesinger's scenario in *The Age of Jackson* portrays the Old Republicans passing on their legacy to such figures as Van Buren and Benton rather than to Calhoun. It should be clear, however, who gave lip service to their ideas and who creatively carried them out. See also Donald F. Swanson, "'Bank-notes Will Be But as Oak Leaves': Thomas Jefferson on Paper Money," in *Virginia Magazine of History and Biography* 101 (Jan.1993): 37-52.

of many radical libertarian Locofocos and moderate independent commercial gentlemen of the North. Not as Marx of the Master Class but as the best representative of a true republican polity.

Though it has never been examined except in passing, a substantial number of labor leaders and libertarian thinkers gave their allegiance to Calhoun. Orestes Brownson's youthful discipleship is well known. Less well known but even more steadfast supporters of this type were Condy Raguet of Philadelphia and Fitzwilliam Byrdsall of New York. Interestingly, these men accepted the South's position not only on economic questions but also on the superiority of southern society to northern in the preservation of liberal principles. They agreed that the South was a necessary restraint to acquisitive mercantilism and deprecated abolition as a form of hypocritical Puritan mania.

This was a constant theme in letters received by Calhoun from sympathizers. One of these, Ellwood Fisher, an Ohio Democratic leader and a Quaker, wrote in the Cincinnati *Enquirer* in 1846 of the moral superiority of slave society to capitalist society: "The money power, like every other kind of power, aims to be paramount and exclusive. It aims at a showy form of civilization of its own ... luxury collected from every clime where money finds its slaves."[10] Raguet (1784-1842) has received some attention from twentieth-century libertarian scholars as an able advocate of free trade and "free banking." It has not been noted that in the several publications he edited, he vehemently defended South Carolina on nullification and repeatedly contrasted the tolerant, gentlemanly virtues of the South to New England WASP prejudice and hypocrisy. (He was of French descent.)[11]

---

10 "John C. Calhoun" by [Ellwood] F[isher], Cincinnati *Enquirer,* as reprinted in the Tallahassee, Fla., *Floridian,* 9 Jan.1847.

11 Raguet's journals were the *Free Trade Advocate and Journal of Political Economy* (Philadelphia, 1829); *Banner of the Constitution* (Washington, D.C., 1829-33); *Examiner, and Journal of Political Economy* (Philadelphia, 1833-35). An extended circle of pro-Calhoun intellectuals in Philadelphia is well described in H. Arthur Scott Trask, "The Constitutional Republicans of Philadelphia, 1818-1848: Hard Money, Free Trade, and State Rights" (Ph.D. diss., University of South Carolina, 1998).

Byrdsall, author of *The History of the Locofoco or Equal Rights Party of New York*, fought hard against both Tammany and Free-Soil Democrats and would write in a typical letter to Calhoun: "In short, my dear Sir, I am satisfied that the salvation of this confederacy from the evils which now beset it, depends entirely upon the Southern States." And again on abolitionists: "The peaceful teachings of the Gospel are abandoned to get up a crusade of falsehood slander dissention disunion throughout the Confederacy, in short the press the pulpit the monarchists the aristocrats the demagogues of Europe and the States are as zealously engaged in the work of wickedness as if they were serving both God & man. And yet they are no friends of the negro. ... He has no real friends but in the Southern States"[12] And again:

> The South is bound by every motive sacred and dear to the heart of man to maintain intact her own social organization, for it is far preferable to that of Europe and the free states. The latter is calculated for nothing so much as the uttermost development of all the selfish properties of human nature. Every man is in competition with his fellow men, to build himself up on the ruin of others ... upon the dog eat dog principle. ... I for one as a member of a Christian church will never consent to change it [the Southern social system] for the heartless, selfish, vice misery and crime producing social system of the North. Besides, such is the intense dislike of the prolétaires toward the non-producers in the free States in consequence of the wealth and luxury which they create but cannot partake or enjoy, that discontent and hatred exists to an extent scarcely imaginable.[13]

Byrdsall told how he had encountered an industrialist who was gleeful over the Mexican War, which he thought would leave a debt of a hundred million dollars and thus compel restoration of a high tariff: "This man is but one of a numerous class whose selfish interests over[r]

---

12 Byrdsall to Calhoun, 7 May, 23 July 1849, Calhoun Papers, Clemson University.
13 Byrdsall to Calhoun, 11 Feb. 1850, Calhoun Papers, SCL.

ule all considerations: of the loss of life ... as well as ... patriotism or common justice. And yet it is very probable that he (as well as most of the class he belongs to) is a member or elder of a Christian church-a praying and hymn singing man."[14]

Calhoun also found allegiance among moderate Whig members of the merchant class, those who agreed with him that national prosperity was a matter of reciprocity rather than ruthless sectional aggrandizement as in the tariff. Charles Augustus Davis, a New York City merchant and well-known writer under the pen name "Major Jack Downing," conducted a long correspondence with Calhoun on the injustice of the tariff, the need for nationally unifying measures, and the willingness of northern capitalists to invest in southern transportation. There were a number of other New York mercantile men who felt the same way.

In response to such supporters, Calhoun was always ready to seek reform gradually in economic matters. Thus in 1834 he said he was willing to extend the charter of the Bank of the United States another six years to allow a gradual transition to another system. In 1842 he actually opposed certain reductions in the tariff because he thought they were politically motivated and would involve the South in reneging on the gradual reductions that had been agreed to in the Compromise of 1833.

Such agreements between the sections were to him morally binding. However, the ineluctable flaw in this approach was that in a system of political operatives and shifting majorities, reciprocity could not be maintained. He was pursuing the impossible, seeking a permanent consensual basis of agreement (as he was later to do on slavery) that was simply not going to be kept by the other side. As Merrill Peterson has pointed out, "Calhoun's whole tendency ... was

---

[14] Byrdsall to Calhoun, 4 Aug. 1846, *Papers of John C. Calhoun* 23:387.

to approach issues theoretically rather than practically and to seek resolution the hard way, on principles, rather than by balancing interests and accommodation to circumstances."[15]

As a part of his strategy of meeting the sensible men of the North halfway and in good faith, Calhoun always blamed bad economic legislation not on businessmen but on politicians. It was the politicians who made the tariff and Bank into issues so polarized and obfuscated that they could not be settled by reason. His scorn for capitalists was muted; that for northern Democratic politicians who supposedly were committed to free trade but in fact voted for tariff bills and engaged in the logrolling for special interests that this involved, was unstinted.

But so thorough was Calhoun's commitment to free trade in principle that he refused to countenance even retaliatory duties. "If other countries injured us by burdensome exactions," he remarked, "it was no reason why we should do harm to ourselves."[16] "Free trade," he said on another occasion in words reminiscent of the late twentieth century, is "destined to work the greatest and most happy change ... Its reaction on politics, morals and religion will be powerful and most salutary." Again, Free trade "is, in my opinion, emphatically the cause of civilization & peace."[17] And he refused to come out for "incidental protection" as a part of a mostly revenue tariff, a political expedient adopted by several Democratic presidential contenders and often urged upon Calhoun by supporters.

It is curious how indifferent historians have been to the South's complaint about the tariff, often dismissing it as a scapegoat for the section's own economic shortcomings or as a disguised form of slavery conflict. But the plain truth is that Calhoun was entirely correct in his opposition to the tariff. Debates about the actual macro and micro-economic effects of antebellum protection are beside the point. The South, providing the bulk of the Union's exports, sold in

---

15 Merrill D. Peterson, *Olive Branch and Sword-The Compromise of 1833* (Baton Rouge, La., 1982), 60.

16 Remarks, 27 Jan. 1841, *Papers of John C. Calhoun* 15:474.

17 To Francis Wharton, 25 Dec. 1843; to the Manchester Anti-Corn Law League, 24 March 1845, *ibid.*, 17:642, 21:445.

an unprotected world market, while all American consumers bought in a highly protected one. And this was to the benefit of one class, no matter how plausibly disguised as a public boon. Such exactions are hard to justify at any time, but especially so in a federal Union in which economic interests are regionalized in such a way that the exploitive effect is concentrated. Americans had fought a revolution for smaller grievances. Not to mention, as Calhoun pointed out in the *South Carolina Exposition,* to the agreement of free traders, that the tariff's "tendency is, to make the poor poorer and the rich richer."

But the tariff, like abolition, was also a question of honour. The disingenuous arguments of the protectionists tended, like those of the abolitionists, to dwell upon the moral inferiority and stupidity of Southerners in comparison with wise, righteous, industrious New Englanders. Calhoun did not engage in that type of polemic, but he replied to it, again in the *Exposition:* "We are told, by those who pretend to understand our interest better than we do, that the excess of production and not the Tariff, is the evil which afflicts us ... We would feel more disposed to respect the spirit in which the advice is offered ... if those from whom it comes accompanied it with the weight of their example. *They* also, occasionally, complain of low prices; but instead of diminishing the supply, as a remedy for the evil, demand an enlargement of the market, by the exclusion of all competition."

Calhoun had supported the tariff of 1816 as a measure of justice to those New Englanders whose interests had been dislocated by government action in Embargo and war. This support was part of his pursuit of harmony and reciprocity. When he was later attacked as inconsistent, he pointed out that he had viewed the tariff of 1816 as temporary. He had not foreseen that it would become a permanent, ever-tightening system, that even after the retirement of the national debt, the duties would not come down.

Given his political inheritance and the clear interest of those he represented, Calhoun could have taken no other position than to view the tariff as oppression and a violation of the bargain of the Union. Had reciprocity been forthcoming from the other side, how different might the course of American history have been. Indeed it is clear that in 1861 a large part of support for the war against the South came from a fear of free trade and the loss of revenue from the South.[18] Condy Raguet had been eloquent about the smooth and ruthless "lobbyists" of the "Yankee" capitalists who haunted the outer rooms of Congress. With the South gone they indeed had the upper hand.

In regard to the public lands, which were the American people's endowment as well as the largest source of government revenue after the tariff, Calhoun made farseeing though unsuccessful legislative efforts. In 1837 he first proposed and later often reintroduced a bill to cede the public lands that remained unsold after ten years on the market to the western states in which they were situated. Some of any future revenue would go to the government, and the lands would still get into the hands of legitimate settlers. The advantages would be to free the federal government from a major source of expense, corruption, and contention and to free the "new states" from vassalage, putting them on the same basis as the "old states" in regard to their lands.

Further, and here we see Calhoun's pursuit of moral and harmonious progress once again, it would be a gesture of generosity from the East to the West that would cement the bonds of Union. It was in the same spirit by which the old states had generously turned over their western claims as a common treasure of the Union.

The hallowed Jeffersonian policy was that the lands be sold off at moderate prices to legitimate settlers, thus obviating the need for direct taxes. During the Jacksonian period two popular contrary ideas took hold. One was the homestead act favored by some Democrats and later taken up by the Republicans with disastrous consequences in the West—give the land away to individuals and to corporations to encourage development ("Vote Yourself a Farm"). The other policy, particularly popular with Whigs, was called "Distribution," by which the revenue derived from sale of public lands would be distributed as a "surplus" to all the states. This was politically popular because all states were to be paid off on the basis of their federal population.

---

18 See Kenneth M. Stampp, *And the War Came: The North and the Secession Crisis, 1860-1861* (Baton Rouge, La.,1950), and the more recent Charles Adams, *For Good and Evil: The Impact of Taxes upon the Course of Civilization* (New York,1992).

These Whig "conservatives" thus would dissipate the public treasury, requiring more taxes (an indirect pressure for a higher tariff) and making the states dependent upon congressional largesse.

To Calhoun such plans were immoral in all aspects-squandering the endowment of the Union, breaking faith with the states that had given up their claims to provide a source of revenue for the government, providing an excuse to raise the tariff, continuing all the expense and corruption inherent in federal administration of the lands, and encouraging states to take on irresponsible debts in the expectation of "a windfall."

A distribution bill passed in 1841 and soon after had to be suspended. The whole project proved a disaster, throwing many states into disgraceful defaults, as Calhoun had predicted. The South Carolina General Assembly, alone among all the states, had refused to accept its portion of the "surplus."

Calhoun's proposal was too simple, too good, to be adopted, requiring as it did the federal politicians to give up certain advantages for the greater good. By Calhoun's plan the western states would have had a secure endowment which they could have used as they wished. The plan would have put the means for internal improvements directly into the treasuries of the states, helping to remove another troublesome and corrupting issue from Congress. Young Abraham Lincoln, then a member of the Illinois legislature, wrote his congressman in enthusiastic support of Calhoun's proposal.[19]

Had Calhoun been successful on this and on other issues, it is possible to imagine a different scenario for some aspects of American history. There would have been some corruption in the states, but nothing that could have matched the vast land giveaways to corporations by the Republicans after 1861. The states and thus genuine federalism would have been measurably strengthened. Calhoun took a statesmanlike and farseeing position, though opposed by the "practical" politicians of both parties.

---

19 Lincoln to John T. Stuart, 1 Jan. 1840, in *The Collected Works of Abraham Lincoln*, ed. Roy P. Basler, 8 vols. (New Brunswick, N.J., 1953), 1:135-38, 181.

Calhoun's earliest peacetime fame came from his relationship to his country's dreams of development and progress. He was, after all, the young patriot who had declared, "Let us conquer space." Calhoun appears with advantage, compared with other leaders of the time, in his efforts, persistently renewed, to make federal internal improvements into a truly constructive and unifying force rather than the egregious example of logrolling they increasingly became as the century wore on.

He contended as a young congressman, as secretary of war, and later, that if the federal government was to engage in subsidy of internal improvements (setting aside the constitutional issue for the moment), there should be a master plan that would truly benefit all of the Union, or at least large regions of it. Whether it was constitutional or not, he added, Congress' never had abandoned the power and never would abandon it.

President Madison had vetoed Calhoun's original plan on his last day in office in 1817, approving the plan but insisting on the need for a constitutional amendment to clarify federal power. Monroe had taken a similar position. John Quincy Adams had scorned constitutional scruples and had failed. Jackson had assumed a presidential prerogative of determining, with the veto, which projects were constitutional and which were not, and had provided no real leadership on the issue, as usual.

In this stalemate of more than three decades, Congress legislated continuously for projects here and there, without any plan that embraced ends "appropriately called federal," in Calhoun's words. It merely responded to the most effective special interests. The expenditures had not been "systematic, judicious, and efficient."[20] If Congress did possess any power in this area, then surely it was for "federal" and not for local objects, Calhoun contended. As usual, many "practical" politicians found Calhoun's "metaphysical" distinction incomprehensible.

---

20 Report on the Memphis Memorial, 26 June 1846, *Papers of John C. Calhoun* 23:193-228.

In 1828, justifying a casting vote as vice president to limit certain appropriations, he remarked:

> "If the system of Internal Improvement cannot be confined, in practice, to objects of really national importance, as contemplated, by the act of 1824; and if it must degenerate into those merely local, having no reference to the powers and duties of the general government, it would, and ought, to fall into disrepute."[21]

It was clear to Calhoun that as a matter of equity and justice, which he always saw in the concept of Union, the demands of the growing West had to be satisfied in some way. The Old Northwest in the 1840s was filling with population around the Great Lakes and was in the midst of unprecedented expansion. Its greatest need was for transportation to markets. And the Southwest had been almost entirely neglected by Congress. The West sooner or later would have its way. Better and wiser to concede generously at once.

In 1843, speaking of the Tennessee River valley, he asked if a Senate committee "would inquire how far this great river was entitled to their attention; and that they would establish some principle upon which the navigation of these great internal seas—for such, to all intents, they were—might be improved."[22]

After serving as president of the Southwestern Commercial Convention in Memphis in 1846, Calhoun undertook to provide the principle himself. What could and ought the general government do in this area that would achieve a relatively wide consensus and serve legitimate "Federal" purposes? His report for a Senate select committee gave his answer. The Congress had clear constitutional power over interstate and foreign commerce. This power was without doubt among those delegated by the states, and it had been construed from the beginning as allowing the government to engage in improvements

---

21 Remarks, 9 April 1828, *ibid.*, 10:369.
22 Remarks, 17 Jan.1843, *ibid.*, 16:614.

of navigation—harbors, lighthouses, and other federally constructed navigational aids dotted the shores of the Atlantic and Gulf coasts and the Great Lakes.

Calhoun reasoned that the Mississippi River and its tributaries were a great inland sea—an artery of an immense volume of interstate and foreign commerce over which no state could exercise jurisdiction. Thus the government could legitimately engage in improvements of navigation in the Mississippi Valley. And for this purpose he introduced a bill to develop a systematic survey. He did not touch on the issue of land transport except to hint that some assistance might be given for roads and railroads (as was in fact already the common practice) by means of defense and mail contracts.

Another proposal had to do with the public lands. Did not the Congress, in its capacity as proprietor and trustee of the public lands, have the right or even the duty to join with the states and private enterprise in encouraging improvements that would enhance the value of the lands and thus the non-tax revenue of the government? Especially when this involved no expenditures but merely donations of some land, as was already the practice, to encourage development and thus increase the value of the rest and the revenue to be derived. Such grants, he stressed, would have to be carefully limited and supervised to prevent exploitation of the public, but judiciously applied on the basis of a master plan, they could be of universal benefit. And he renewed his suggestion that unsold lands be turned over to the western states. This practice would both bolster the dignity of the states and provide them with a source of development capital. And, Calhoun pointed out, Congress itself was responsible for hindrances to development: tariff protection for Pennsylvania iron interests added $2,000 per mile to the costs of railroad construction.

Calhoun's 1846 plan failed of adoption. Instead the Congress passed an immense logrolling "rivers and harbors" bill with forty-nine local projects, mostly for the Midwest. President Polk properly vetoed this, on good constitutional and expedient grounds. However, as Calhoun pointed out, Polk and his party provided no leadership on the issue— no alternative to satisfy legitimate demands. One can reasonably argue that this event, along with the 1846 tariff reductions, began the unraveling of Democratic strength and the rise of Free-Soilism in the Midwest and the mid-Atlantic states and thus led inevitably to the eventual crack-up of the Union. Suppose Calhoun's conciliatory program had been adopted, dampening down the northern belief that southern politicians thwarted the North's legitimate interests?

Two questions can only be touched on briefly here: Calhoun's opposition to a federal bankruptcy law and his guarding of the treasury from unnecessary expenditures. His great speech of 2 June 1840, against a proposed federal bankruptcy act—which was essentially a form of bailout for banks and other corporations-is an eloquent argument against the abandonment of public virtue for special interests.

And for his fifteen years in the Senate, Calhoun was on the watch for expenditures that were unnecessary or unauthorized. Though he always maintained that those things the government had a duty to do, it should do, well, time and again he pointed out that expenditures which seemed plausible or appealed to the sympathies of legislators created unwholesome precedents, exceeded Congress's authority, and, most importantly, involved an abuse of the people's labour. Like the tariff, such actions invariably transferred wealth from one group to another and so should be kept at a minimum. "We robbed the People in levying taxes. It was plunder and nothing more, and reform and retrenchment could be accomplished in no other way than correcting the erroneous doctrines which had grown up." "Economy and accountability," he said on another occasion, "are virtues belonging to free and popular Governments, and without which they cannot long endure."[23] His defense of the agrarian version of republican virtue never wavered, and many Americans, North and South, honoured him for the consistency of principle.

Money is that great Mystery the love of which is near universal and the root of all evil. One needs only to think of "Not worth a Continental," "the Monster Bank," "the Cross of Gold," and beyond, to be reminded

---

23 See Clyde N. Wilson, ed., *The Essential Calhoun* (New Brunswick, N.J., 1992), 163-88, esp. 183-84, 187.

of the large and controversial part it has played in American political history. Historians in general have seen the recurrent conflicts over money largely in terms of capitalist/agrarian and creditor/debtor conflict. Much discussion has rested on the empirically false assumption (apparently derived from the late nineteenth-century battles over bimetallism) that capitalists are always in favor of "hard money" and agrarians always in favor of inflation or "cheap money." The actualities are quite a bit more complicated because capitalists, or some of them, have often been in the forefront of promoting currency expansion and inflation. Money is indeed a great Mystery, not only involving the interest of every member of society but surrounded by strong emotions and (often man-made) clouds of confusion.

Calhoun perhaps appears in his best light as a national statesman when we follow his course through the banking and currency conflicts of his time. It is difficult, I think, to find here the mere sectional politician that so many wish to see him to be.

Financial disarray brought on by the War of 1812 and the difficulties of financing the war led the Madison administration to revive the idea of a national bank. The first United States Bank of Hamilton, which the Republican party had come into existence opposing, had expired in 1811. Calhoun, as an administration leader in the House of Representatives, was asked to manage the bill to revive the Bank, a task he accepted, feeling strongly the obligation that he, as an advocate of the declaration of war, had to achieve good results. "This" Calhoun later observed, "was *my* first lesson on banks. It has made a durable impression on my mind."

When he looked at the plan. "I had not proceeded far before I was struck with the extraordinary character of the subject; a bank of $50,000,000, whose capital was to consist almost exclusively of Government credit in the shape of stock ... to furnish the Government with loans to carry on the war! I saw at once that the effect of the arrangement would be, that the Government would borrow back its own credit, and pay six per cent per annum for what they had already paid eight or nine."[24] Calhoun had put his finger on the bottom line of modern government finance, the alliance of government and great capital that had been designed by Hamilton.

Yet how else deal with the existing "embarrassment of the Treasury" when the Bank was the only remedy on the table: "I cast my eyes around, and soon saw that the Government should use its own credit directly, without the intervention of a bank; which I proposed to do in the form of Treasury notes, to be issued in the operations of the Government, and to be funded in the subscription to the stock of the bank."[25]

The chartering of the Second Bank of the United States was a complicated struggle extending over several sessions of Congress, but Calhoun was generally considered the rightful father of the bill, it having been extensively amended by him to ensure that "the capital of the bank should consist of funded Treasury notes; and that instead of a mere paper machine, it should be a specie-paying bank, so as to be an ally instead of an opponent in restoring the currency to a sound condition."[26]

Treasury notes were paper issued by the government in payment of its expenditures. They were receivable in payment of government obligations, as at the customhouses and land offices, and were redeemable in specie, usually after the passage of one year. A great many things intersected here, in Calhoun's observation. For the rest of his career he advocated in the case of all government expenditures, the use of Treasury notes. Why should the government go into the market to borrow money at high rates, with no risk to the lender, when it could issue its own currency? (Interestingly, the same Whigs, like Webster, who regarded a debt as a blessing and advocated loans, attacked Calhoun's issues of Treasury notes as piling up a dangerous debt!)

---

24 Speech, 3 Oct. 1837, *Papers of John C. Calhoun* 13:609, 612.

25 *Ibid.*, 610.

26 *Ibid.*, 611. The "inconsistent" and "opportunistic" Calhoun made exactly the same proposals thirty years later on the financing of the Mexican War. See Remarks of 18 July and 4 Aug. 1846, *ibid.*, 23:335-36, 391-92.

Calhoun had observed that the soundness and acceptability of the notes made them a circulating medium. Because they were known to be sound, they did not have to be redeemed but could circulate in the private economy as a currency. This not only was a boon to the government, saving interest charges, but went far toward meeting the Congress's constitutional obligation: to provide the currency of the country in the absence of a sufficient amount of specie and given the inconvenience of coin.

In 1832, responding to a variety of ideas and impulses, Andrew Jackson vetoed Henry Clay's early renewal of the Second Bank of the United States' twenty-year charter, which was to expire in 1836. Then Jackson's Treasury Department withdrew the government funds from their legal resting place in the Bank and put them into a variety of private, state-chartered banks picked by his own administration. This withdrawal inaugurated a struggle between advocates and opponents of a National Bank that seesawed back and forth until the Civil War triumph of the Republican party. During this struggle Calhoun pursued an independent and elevated course.

In the Senate, Calhoun analyzed with merciless logic and clarity the illegality and sophistry of Jackson's proceedings and supported Clay's resolutions of censure. Whatever the faults of the Bank, it had acted, on the whole, responsibly, and 'it was the law. The "pet banks" that now held the government funds were a vast spoils system which the executive had created for itself and a danger to the economy as well.

Thus far he agreed with the Whigs. But in a great speech of 21 March 1834, he indicated that although an opponent of Jackson's proceedings, he was no longer an advocate of a Bank of the United States, though he was willing to see it continue for a few more years to provide a gradual transition.

He presented a history of banking, indicating the study he had put into the subject since 1816, and put his finger on the real issue. It was not a question of Bank or no Bank but a question of the control of the currency. Even with the Bank of the United States out of the picture, the government was still deeply involved with the banking system. Why? Because Alexander Hamilton, in a little-noticed executive order, which had been casually validated by 1816 legislation, had begun accepting the notes issued by banks as if they were equivalent to specie. Since then the banking system had grown exponentially. On the one hand, the Bank of the United States had some control over the banks in that it could regulate their practices by receiving their notes at various degrees below face value. On the other hand, the banks made use of the government's validation to back their paper. People, observed Calhoun, still thought of banks largely as places of deposit and had not noticed the explosion of "banks of discount," what was later to be called "fractional reserve banking." The banks now had vast power to expand or contract the credit of the country by the issuing of notes.

The banks were lending far out of proportion to their specie reserves, thus creating what would later be called the business cycle—boom followed by bust. (Calhoun accurately predicted the panic of 1837 three years in advance.) Jackson's actions had greatly aggravated the situation, encouraging the pet banks to even greater expansion and removing the power of the Bank of the United States to curb them.

Calhoun noted issues that were being neglected in the smoke and din of party warfare over the Bank. It was the Congress's constitutional duty to provide a sound circulating medium. There was no reason this duty had to be performed by delegating power to a national bank. The states were forbidden by the Constitution to emit bills of credit, but state-chartered private institutions had been encouraged by the federal government to do what the states were forbidden to do and thus were performing the duty of Congress. Further, control of the currency and credit of the country was the most powerful instrument that had ever been developed for transferring wealth from one group to another. Currency of all sorts made up only one-twenty-fifth or one-thirtieth of the wealth of the country, "and yet this small proportion of the property of the community regulates the value of all the rest, and forms the medium of circulation by which all its exchanges are effected."

He added:

Place the money power in the hands of a single individual, or a combination of individuals, and, by expanding or contracting the currency, they may raise or sink prices at pleasure; and ... may command the whole property and industry of the community, and control its fiscal operations. The banking system concentrates and places this power in the hands of those who control it, and its force increases just in proportion as it dispenses with a metallic basis. Never was an engine invented better calculated to place the destiny of the many in the hands of the few, or less favorable to that equality and independence which lie at the bottom of all free institutions.[27]

In 1836 Calhoun played a leading role in forming and passing a Deposit Act which regulated and legalized the pet bank system—forcing the banks to pay for the privilege of using the government funds and guarding against the fraud and defaults that had taken place. In addition, the act provided for surplus treasury funds to be distributed to the states rather than held in the banks for their use. Calhoun approved of this distribution, which was not linked to the sales of public lands but was aimed at disposing of the huge surplus created by the tariffs of 1828 and 1832.

In defending this provision he pointed out that the Jacksonians, who called themselves the friends of the people, had shown no hesitancy in distributing public funds among favored banks and public lands among favored speculators but were opposing the distribution of the surplus to the states: "Were they to leave it with the banks, as an instrument for political purposes? Why should gentlemen recommend so extraordinary a course, so unequal, so partial, to avoid returning it to the people to whom it belonged? Why were they so averse to such a distribution? Was it to prevent the people from being corrupted? Were

---

27 *Ibid.*, 602.

the people alone capable of being corrupted? Were the Government and banks all pure, while the people, the people alone, were corrupt and corruptible?"[28]

On 18 September and 3 October 1837, Calhoun made in the Senate two great speeches supporting the Independent Treasury or Subtreasury plan that Van Buren had put forward. Thus he put aside his opposition to Van Buren and rejoined the Democratic party for the national crisis of the panic. And he expanded his analysis of the history and nature of banking.

It was time, Calhoun maintained, that Congress directly undertook its constitutional responsibility over the currency and separated the government and the currency from private privilege, profit, and control. But it was necessary not only to set up the Independent Treasury. This did not really divorce the government from the banks as long as the government accepted and dealt in the notes issued by private state-chartered banks. He offered an amendment to the Independent Treasury that would have gradually eliminated the government's reception of banknotes, which involved the government in support of the banks and their power over the credit supply of the country. He desired to separate the government and the banks and let each go its own way. (Thus the slogan "Separation from Banks.") The market would regulate banknotes without the artificial support of the government. His amendment to this effect passed. The Independent Treasury passed the Senate but failed to be acted on in the House at that time, though it was established in 1846.

Calhoun's economic analysis, I would argue, reflected brilliant insight and high statesmanship. He cut through the demagoguery and superficiality of political conflict in an attempt to discern the public good. And his arguments always came back to the ethics of the community—the moral degradation and the undermining of republican virtue that resulted from interested legislative manipulations. The alliance of bankers and government was an imposition on honest farmers and merchants, a threat to their independence and to the moral climate

---

28 Remarks, 28 Feb. 1837, *ibid.*, 13:480.

that was necessary to sustain free government. His eloquence on these matters is still moving. Calhoun once remarked, "I do not hesitate to say, if Genl. Hamilton had not issued his circular directing bank notes to be received as gold & silver in the publick dues, and if the Bank of the United States had not been created, the whole course of politics under our system would have been entirely different."[29] Another time he declared, "It has justly been stated by a British writer that the power to make a small piece of paper, not worth one cent, by the inscribing of a few names, to be worth a thousand dollars, was a power too high to be entrusted to the hands of mortal man."[30]

Hear Calhoun on the moral effects of the banking system:

> If a community be so organized as to cause a demand for high mental attainments, they are sure to be developed. If its honours and rewards are allotted to pursuits that require their development by creating a demand for intelligence, knowledge, wisdom, justice, firmness, courage, patriotism, and the like, they are sure to be produced. But, if allotted to pursuits that require inferior qualities, the higher are sure to decay and perish. I object to the banking system, because it allots the honors and rewards of the community, in a very undue proportion, to a pursuit the least of all others favorable to the development of the higher mental qualities, intellectual or moral, to the decay of the learned professions, and the more noble pursuits of science, literature, philosophy, and statesmanship, and the great and more useful pursuits of business and industry. With the vast increase of its profits and influence, it is gradually concentrating in it itself most of the prizes of life ... The rising generation cannot but feel its deadening influence.[31]

---

29 To James H. Hammond, 16 May 1840, *ibid.*, 15:228-29.
30 Remarks, 29 Dec.1841, *ibid.*, 16:25.
31 Speech, 3 Oct.1837, *ibid.*, 13:603.

Calhoun demonstrates thoroughly what Eugene Genovese writes of the slave-holding class: that they "did place great weight on the quantitative progress of morality and did see material progress as its handmaiden." Many historians have attributed to them, therefore, a "basically bourgeois worldview to which they merely tacked on an opportunistic defense of slave property." Of such historians, Genovese remarks, "They err."[32]

Forrest McDonald has ascribed to the Founding Fathers two different versions of republicanism.[33] Puritanical republicanism saw the state as the instrument of promoting and preserving virtue. The agrarian republicanism of the South relied upon independence of the citizen for the preservation of virtue and regarded the government as an enemy to be watched and limited. The triumph of puritanical republicanism has been nearly complete, though it has shifted its emphasis from material progress to distribution and more, lately to political correctness. The type of discourse represented by Calhoun has all but disappeared from the American public dialogue and perhaps not all for the good.

Calhoun was the chief public man of the Old South, and his economics were the South's. Those things in which the Confederate Constitution differed from the United States Constitution were provisions governing the economic behavior of government, along the lines Calhoun had laid down. Interestingly enough, the two constitutions differed hardly at all on the question of slavery.

Calhoun's philosophy represented the last gasp of agrarian republicanism of which only the faintest echoes remain in the American consciousness. But it also represented an effort to adapt that ideology to the prospects of material and moral progress of the nineteenth century without sacrificing it, and also to adapt it to the more organic concepts of man and society that appeared in the post-Enlightenment era. This

---

32 Eugene Genovese, *The Slaveholders' Dilemma: Freedom and Progress in Southern Conservative Thought, 1820-1860* (Columbia, S.C., 1992), 33.

33 Forrest McDonald, *Novus Ordo Seclorum: The Intellectual Origins of the Constitution* (Lawrence, Kans., 1985), 70-77.

intellectual effort took place, as the works of Eugene Genovese have so profoundly demonstrated, in a society necessarily committed to the defense of its unique historical burden of slavery.

From Slavery, Secession and Southern History,
edited by Robert Louis Paquette. University Press of Virginia, 2000.
Published by permission.

JOHN C. CALHOUN: ANTI-IMPERIALIST
"A WISE AND MASTERLY INACTIVITY"

THE DOMINANT POWERS in American discourse today have succeeded in confining the South to a dark little corner of history labeled "Slavery and Treason." This is already governing the public sphere of the Civil War Sesquicentennial. Such an approach not only libels the South, it is a fatal distortion of of American history in general, and, I dare say, even of African-American history. The old Radical Republican propaganda that portrays John C. Calhoun as a scheming fanatic who brought on civil war by his determination to spread slavery has re-emerged. A little over a half century ago, the historiographical picture was quite different. Margaret Coit's admiring biography won a Pulitzer Prize.[1] A leading expert on the subject wrote that Calhoun understood the mysteries of banking and money better than anyone else at the time.[2] Numerous scholars, mostly of a liberal and progressive disposition, praised Calhoun's concurrent majority as a brilliant and useful concept.[3] A United States Senate Committee chaired by John F. Kennedy named Calhoun one of the five greatest Senators of all time.

One is tempted to conclude that historical knowledge is not cumulative and to agree with Orwell that who controls the present controls the past, and who controls the past controls the future. Certainly the present discourse reflects not historical judgment but a political/ideological agenda.

---

1   *John C. Calhoun: American Portrait* (Boston: Houghton Mifflin, 1950).

2   Bray Hammond, *Banks and Politics in America: From the Revolution to the Civil War* (Princeton NJ: Princeton University Press, 1957), pp. 37, 111, 234 – 237, 368, 427 – 429, 609.

3   For a few examples: Peter F. Drucker, "A Key to American Politics: Calhoun's Pluralism," *Review of Politics* 10 (October 1948), pp. 412 – 426; Felix Morley, *Freedom and Federalism* (Chicago: Henry Regnery, 1951); Ralph Lerner, "Calhoun's New Science of Politics," *American Political Science Quarterly* 57 (December 1963), pp. 918 – 932; David M. Potter, *The South and the Concurrent Majority* (Baton Rouge: Louisiana State University Press, 1972).

In the Jacksonian era, so-called, I have learned that one must not only look for political bias, one must look for comic book versions of history. One noted historian of the period, who has appeared often on television as a savant, once asked me to verify a quotation about Henry Clay often attributed to Calhoun. Calhoun is supposed to have said something like "Henry Clay is a scoundrel, but, by God, I love him." You don't have to spend much time with Calhoun to understood that both the language and the opinion are phony. With much work I found the origin of the quotation. It was in a dubious memoir published in 1880 by a social butterfly (male) who claimed to know everybody of importance.,[4] I provided the historian in question with three authentic remarks by Calhoun about Clay, all more interesting than the spurious one. When the book was published I found the same phony material used. I assume because it fits in with his imaginary version of the times that the author wished to portray.

This same writer, in another very well-received book, vividly describes John C. Calhoun grinding his teeth in chagrin because he has been out-witted by Martin Van Buren. How could he possibly know this? What possible benefit to historical understanding is conveyed? Martin Van Buren may have considered politics as a game of wits between different personalities, but Calhoun did not. Historians relentlessly purvey the charge, originating in demagogurey of the times, that Calhoun's actions are explained by his thwarted ambition to be President. Does such ambition describe a man who broke with President Jackson over a matter of honour, resigned as Vice-President to defend his State, opposed Jackson without joining the opposition party that wanted to claim him, and raised a lonely voice against the Mexican War which threatened his popularity in the South and even in South Carolina? Calhoun understood the American political system better than most, and he knew perfectly well in the last 20 years of

---

[4] Henry Wikoff, *Reminiscences of an Idler* (New York: Fords, Howard & Hulbert, 1880).

his life that he could never be President, and did not much care. If supporters wanted to keep his name out there, that was good, because it enhanced his weight in matters that he did care about.[5]

Calhoun was a major figure very near the pinnacle of American statecraft for forty years. His influence, though never dominant, even in the South, was Union-wide. It was largely moral and intellectual and extended to many more subjects than the sectional conflict. Which is why ambitious politicians of all parties hated him and attempted to reduce his standing by cheap ridicule which some historians continue to retail.[6] Several writers have put forth the proposition that a statesman differs from a politician in that a statesman perceives the long-range consequences of actions, lays out for a society its real alternatives, and, though he usually goes unheard, warns of future dangers. By this rule, Calhoun was indeed a statesman. All politicians and many historians imagine than nothing exists higher than a politician.

In an article in a collection in honour of Eugene Genovese I briefly described Calhoun's knowledge and statesmanship in regard to economics.[7] A perceptive reviewer was kind enough to say that the article "plowed new ground by the acre."[8] So far, nobody has appeared to plant the ground, and perhaps they never will.

This is my opportunity to do the same for Calhoun on diplomacy and war, where his wisdom, I think, will prove him to have been prophetic. He played a significant role in American diplomacy and war through his entire forty-year career, although a standard diplomatic history of the United States devotes only a few lines to him in passing.

---

5   Clyde N. Wilson et al., eds., *The Papers of John C. Calhoun*, 28 vols. (Columbia University of South Carolina Press, 1959 — 2003), vol. 17, pp. xxiv — xxv. (Hereinafter *Calhoun Papers*).

6   Silly statements that Calhoun was a "cast-iron man," that he began his love letters with "Whereas...," and that "When Mr. Calhoun took snuff, South Carolina sneezed."

7   "Free Trade: No Debt: Separation from Banks': The Economic Platform of John C. Calhoun," in Robert Louis Paquette, ed., *Slavery, Secession, and Southern History* (Charlottesville: University Press of Virginia, 2000), pp. 81–100.

8   *Mississippi Quarterly* 54 (Spring 2001), p. 282.

His acts and words in regard to war are significant, and, since Calhoun is in many ways a definitive Southerner, will help us understand an aspect of the Southern mind.

Let us begin with the "War Hawk" of 1811– 1816. Calhoun's first recorded political speech was at a public meeting in Abbeville in 1807 at which he presented and passed resolutions demanding a forceful response to the *Chesapeake* and *Leopard* affair. This was not what we are familiar with now—not a peevish demand that the government do something. It was an expression of the willingness of South Carolina to fight for American honour.[9] He arrived at the House of Representatives in 1811, and after his first speech, at the age of 29, the leading Jeffersonian editor of the country called him "one of those master spirits who leave their stamp upon the age in which they live."[10] Calhoun spoke eloquently for firm and effective response to British hostility and insults. He drafted the resolution embodying the declaration of war when it came. His labour in the House to bring support to the army and morale to the country during the discouraging times that followed led an editor once more to praise him as "the young Hercules who carried the war on his shoulders."

Calhoun's rhetoric as War Hawk is informative. He never appealed to desire for new territory or seldom even for commercial redress, though that was worthy of attention. He spoke often, and almost always he spoke of the war in terms of honour. The young country could not submit to a bully. To do so would be to forfeit respect and invite further affront. Americans must have the spirit and the means to repel dangers so they could go about their real business.[11]

The war was far from a great success, beginning with the Connecticut Yankee, General William Hull, surrendering the Michigan Territory to the British without even firing a shot. Calhoun had his work cut out for him. Fortunately, the war ended on a high note with

---

9   *Calhoun Papers*, vol. 1, pp. 34—37.
10 Thomas Ritchie in the *Richmond Enquirer*, 24 Dec 1811.
11 *Calhoun Papers*, vol. 1, *passim*.

Jackson's victory at New Orleans, which was achieved by volunteers from nearby Southern States with little thanks due to the government in Washington.

The mess of the war was critical for Calhoun's later thinking. One recent biographer, of the comic book school, suggests that Calhoun was so badly shaken and scared by the failures in the war that his opposition to war thereafter was a matter of fear and an inferiority complex. This biographer also states that he ignores Calhoun's political thought, which he cannot understand and does not think is significant. This biography is so bad that it of course won a prize.[12]

Calhoun's response was positive and constructive. In 1817 he accepted President Monroe's invitation to become Secretary of War. Everyone advised against it. Friends said he would lose his place in national attention, make enemies, and take on an impossible job that would surely end in discredit. Others said Calhoun was too philosophical to be an administrator. Calhoun applied his genius to the problems of the defense of a farflung and growing Union. He went to work to make things better. This is another way you can tell a statesman from a politician. A politician does not work. He spends his time posing for attention and on backstairs maneuvers for advantage.

While other ambitious men were posturing for position, Calhoun devoted his years from age 35 to 42 in a grueling but necessary job that would benefit every part of the Union. It is reasonable to say that Calhoun in his seven years in the War Department did more to create the peacetime U.S. Army than any other single individual.[13]

The largest department of the government was literally in a shambles of accounts and accountability. Calhoun instituted a bureau system that is said to have been copied in Europe. The non-combat branches of the army—engineers, commissary, quartermaster,

---

12 John Niven, *John C. Calhoun and the Price of Union: A Biography* (Baton Rouge: Louisiana State University Press, 1988).

13 There is a large literature dealing with various aspects of Calhoun's administration of the War Department. This period of his career is covered extensively, along with notes to the literature and sources, in *Calhoun Papers*, introductions to vols. 2–6.

ordnance, medical, and Indian Affairs—became efficient. Incidentally, Calhoun acted upon the idea that most troubles with the Indians resulted from the corrupt and incompetent officials sent by the government to deal with them. Later, in the Senate, he vigorously opposed Jackson's Indian removals.

Most importantly, Calhoun provided a Jeffersonian solution to the problems of defense—the expansible army. Americans were hardy and patriotic men who could quickly become good soldiers in an emergency. A large, expensive, and possibly dangerous standing army was not required. What was needed was a core of logistical organisation and professional officers who could organise, supply, train, and lead volunteers when needed. An important key to this was West Point, the prestige of which dates from Calhoun's tenure. The institution was reformed with the best faculty and curriculum available. For a long time West Point was one of the best colleges in the U.S. and certainly the best technical college.

One of his arguments for West Point he had already presented while still in the House, in order to refute the common charge that such an institution would create an aristocratic, unrepublican officer class. The military academy, rather, fit a Jeffersonian educational ideal—to rescue talent from the lower orders. The institution would attract young men who were able and ambitious but without family or money. Not all the graduates would make a career in the small peacetime army. After a few years service they would enter civil life where their training would be of great value to a developing country, and from whence they could return to the colours when called.[14]

While still in the House, Calhoun had drawn up a plan of "internal improvements." This was a masterfully designed system of roads and waterways needed to get men and supplies quickly to threatened points, based entirely on the Constitutional right and duty to provide for the common defense. President Madison found it a good plan but said that a Constitutional amendment was needed to allow it. When Calhoun later opposed "internal improvements" legislation, petty

---

14 *Calhoun Papers*, vol. 1, pp. 287–290.

politicians said he had reversed himself. There was no inconsistency because "internal improvements" legislation had devolved into log-rolling and patronage without any system or any relation to rightful federal powers.

Note that all of his plans contemplated a defensive policy only. He did not foresee that the Union would ever have any need for aggression.

Calhoun survived despite rocky conflicts with Congress and false accusations of fiscal misdeeds cooked up by his cabinet associate and presidential rival William H. Crawford. He emerged from the War Department to be easily elected Vice President in 1824 in an election which split the presidential results four ways—the youngest man ever put so near the White House. Despite all, he never overcame the suspicion of the Old Republicans that he was too much of a nationalist. They had already given up on Union with the North while Calhoun was trying to promote fairness and harmony among its disparate parts. Not until he began to pay close attention to the tariff did he realize that fairness was not reciprocated by dominant Northern interests.

From assuming office as Vice-President in 1825 until his appointment as Secretary of State in 1844, Calhoun was most concerned with internal issues, but established a recognized position on diplomacy and war that was praised by some and deplored by others. In 1836, Jackson sent Congress a message bristling with saber-rattling threats against France in regard to some long-standing unpaid claims. Calhoun's comments in the Senate showed that he knew a good deal more about the issue, and about French politics, than the President or Secretary of State, and described several missed opportunities for settlement. To threaten a major power was the surest possible way to guarantee non-compliance, he said. And one day of war would cost more than the entire sum at issue. The President was going about things all wrong.[15]

---

15 *Calhoun Papers*, vol. 13, pp. 33—41.

Was this inconsistent with the War Hawk of earlier years, and merely expressive of venom against Jackson, as the prize-winning biographer would have it? I don't think so. In 1811 Great Britain was a genuine threat on our coast and our northern border. France in 1836 was not such a case. In fact, in 1811 Calhoun had told the House:

> A bullying menacing system has everything to condemn and nothing to recommend it—in expense it is almost as considerable as war—it excites contempt abroad, and destroys confidence here. Menaces are serious things, and, if we expect any good from them, they ought to be resorted to with as much caution and seriousness as war itself; and should, if not successful, be invariably followed by it.[16]

A characteristic Southern attitude, I think. If you have been injured, don't bluster about retaliation. Issue your challenge soberly and courteously, be open to apology, and be ready to back up your words. Col. David Crockett, the frontier hero, supposedly had a rule: "Be sure you're right, then go ahead!" The "be sure you are right" part is important, the difference between a just man and a bully. You will never, ever, hear this anywhere else, but Col. Crockett was an admirer of Calhoun and not of Jackson.[17]

In similar fashion, Calhoun supported ratification of the Webster-Ashburton Treaty in 1842. It settled most of the Canadian boundary and left in place the standing agreement for joint U.S.-British occupancy of the huge Oregon Territory that had been adopted in 1818. There were many in Congress and the newspapers who were making militant demands for immediate settlement of the Oregon question on American terms.

---

16 *Calhoun Papers*, vol. 1, pp. 75–76.
17 *Calhoun Papers*, vol. 27, p. 484.

These demands would lead two years later to the Democratic campaign slogan "54 40' or fight!"—a declaration of intent that all of the territory, including what is now British Columbia, up to the Russian border in Alaska, shall be American and not British.

In speeches on this question Calhoun described his vision of the American future. The British were not known to bow to threats. The world was growing more enlightened and comfortable. A war between two great powers would be retrograde for civilisation. He pointed out that a quiet delay was all to the American advantage. Our people were ever enterprising. Give them a little time and they would fill up all the North American territory we could reasonably want and make it de facto American. Was this not preferable to war with the greatest power in the world over a yet sparsely settled territory? Further, he said:

> I am finally opposed to war, because peace—peace is pre-eminently our policy. There may be nations, restricted to small territories, hemmed in on all sides, so situated that war may be necessary to their greatness. Such is not our case. Providence has given us an inheritance stretching across the entire continent, from East to West, from ocean to ocean, and from North to South, covering by far the greater and better part of its temperate zone. It comprises a region not only of vast extent, but abundant in all resources; excellent in climate; fertile and exuberant in soil, capable of sustaining, in the plentiful enjoyment of all the necessaries of life, a population ten times our present number. Our great mission, as a people, is to occupy this vast domain; to replenish it with an intelligent, virtuous, and industrious population …. War would but impede the fulfillment of this high mission, by absorbing the means and diverting the energies which would be devoted to the purpose. On the contrary, secure peace, and time, under the guidance of

a sagacious and cautious policy, "a wise and masterly inactivity," will speedily accomplish the whole.[18]

Keep the peace and allow American enterprise to flourish by keeping the federal government confined to "the few great objects for which it was instituted," and "a scene of prosperity and happiness would follow heretofore unequaled on the globe." Calhoun's appeal for "a wise and masterly inactivity" came in for a good deal of ridicule from politicians and press. It is perhaps a natural human tendency to feel that aggressiveness is necessary for advancement. And military success exercises a strong appeal.

I can well imagine those numerous writers who blame the South for every bad thing in American history jumping to the conclusion that Calhoun by these remarks has declared in favour of American exceptionalism, and is therefore guilty of instigating our foreign expeditions to spread democracy. No. He makes an upbeat description of the American potential, but it is the potential for Americans, not for the world, and is spoken in the interest of peace. Compare these words written by the alleged conservative realist John Adams in his diary as early as 1765: "I always consider the settlement of America with reverence and wonder, as the opening of a grand scheme and design in Providence for the illumination of the ignorant, and the emancipation of the slavish part of mankind all over the earth." We have in the contrast an illumination of the Southern tradition and the real source of messianic American exceptionalism—New England.

Calhoun left the Senate in 1843 with the intent of staying at home and working on his farming and his treatise on government. In Washington, on 28 February, 1844, Secretary of State Upshur was killed in an accidental explosion during an excursion on a warship. A week later, without Calhoun's knowledge, President Tyler sent his name to the Senate to be Secretary of State. The nomination was confirmed in a few hours without a single dissent, even from the antislavery Senators of Vermont. Most of the nominations made by Tyler, who was supported by neither party, were routinely rejected. This must tell us

---

18 *Calhoun Papers*, vol. 22, pp. 701–702. See also vol. 16, pp. 393ff.

something about Calhoun's standing as a statesman and his reputation as a peacemaker, for the country faced the most serious questions in foreign affairs since the War of 1812—Texas and Oregon.

Secretary of State Calhoun pursued a peaceful settlement of the Oregon question that would make a division of the territory along the present border. Later, in the Senate, Calhoun defended this approach, pointing out the lunacy of brinkmanship with the strongest power on earth, Brittania ruling the waves, over a territory where the U.S. could neither raise nor support an army. When Polk took over, after two years of blustering he was forced to face reality, give up "54 40' or fight!," and settle on a treaty along the lines Calhoun had laid out.

Some Northerners complained that while Calhoun was eager to bring the Southern territory of Texas into the Union, he was willing to give away Northern territory. But the questions were not the same. Texas had already shown the ability to defend itself, and Mexico, unlike Great Britain, could inflict little harm on the United States. The desire to have Texas in the Union had been thwarted for ten years because of fear of war and because an increasing number of people had been led to believe that when Northerners moved west it was a noble mission to civilise a continent and when Southerners moved west it was an evil conspiracy to spread slavery. The latter situation was due largely to John Quincy Adams's belief that the South had to be destroyed in order to fulfill the New England mission for American greatness.

In 1843-44 Texas had agents in Europe talking with Britain and France about the possibility of defensive alliance. We now know that this was less serious than it seemed at the time. Influential British forces were already moving to extend their worldwide emancipation campaign to Texas. British influence in Texas would give them a much-desired alternative cotton supply and make the Gulf of Mexico into a British lake, threatening American security and Southern society. Following a policy that Tyler had already initiated, Calhoun negotiated a treaty with the Texas Republic by which it would be annexed to the United States. The treaty failed the necessary two-thirds majority in the Senate. Historians have almost unanimously said the defeat came because Calhoun had described the treaty as a necessary measure against foreign abolitionism. This was probably a tactical mistake, but Tyler and Calhoun accomplished part of what they had intended, which was to illuminate British machinations. The conventional interpretation seems to miss the point. Rejection of the treaty was a party vote. The Whigs had a majority and all but one of them voted nay.

This business was naturally pertinent to the 1844 presidential campaign. The prospective Whig candidate Clay and the Democratic front-runner Van Buren happened to cross paths at Raleigh on the campaign trail. They colluded to deal with the explosive issue of Texas by not discussing it at all. This was the kind of political gamesmanship that Calhoun despised and believed was undermining American republicanism. He always advocated putting the issues plainly before the people. This was one of the reasons he confronted abolitionism frankly when most politicians of both parties accused him of agitation because they wanted to pretend a serious issue did not exist.[19]

By bringing Texas prominently into public attention, Tyler and Calhoun eliminated Van Buren from the running so that the Democratic nomination went to the dark-horse James K. Polk, expansionist. And when Polk won his slim victory Congress admitted Texas to the Union by a majority of both houses, avoiding the treaty process.

It was widely expected that Polk would continue Calhoun as Secretary of State. He was, after all, in the midst of dealing with two important questions. Calhoun had the measure of Polk and knew better. If such a Cabinet were to meet, wherever Calhoun sat would be the head of the table, something Polk was not about to accept. He offered Calhoun the post of Minister to Great Britain, which he knew would be turned down.[20]

Texas now was part of the Union. Mexico did not acknowledge this, and further insisted that the southern border of Texas was not at the Rio Grande but at the Nueces a hundred miles further north. The area

---

19 *Calhoun Papers*, vol. 17, p. 52.
20 *Calhoun Papers*, vol. 22, pp. ix–x.

in dispute was semi-arid and occupied mainly by wild longhorns. Polk sent the army to the Rio Grande. Inevitably, American and Mexican patrols ran into each other and fought.

When the news finally reached Washington, Polk's message to Congress said that American blood has been shed on American soil and that a state of war existed. Two days of Congressional wrangling and reluctance followed until both houses adopted, instead of a declaration of war, a resolution recognising the existence of war.

I have said that Calhoun was a prophet. Judge for yourselves. I think you will find that what he has to say about the war with Mexico is just as significant today as it was a century and a half ago.[21]

Calhoun was on his feet at once to criticise. The U.S. and Mexico were at war but there had been no declaration, though this was required by the constitutions of both governments. War should be a considered and deliberate commitment, backed by the people. There were no stated war aims, which made hostilities limitless. Further, what had happened, a border incident, did not necessarily call for all out war, and might be handled in ways short of that.

Worst of all, the President had in effect instigated armed conflict by his action. If this were allowed, then a precedent was set by which any future executive could provoke an incident and commit the country to war by his own decision. Sound familiar? Fort Sumter? "Remember the Maine?" Pearl Harbour? Gulf of Tonkin? "Weapons of mass destruction?" A basic distinction between American republicanism and the monarchical practices of the Old World had been obliterated. The war resolution passed with only a handful of dissenting votes in either house. Calhoun sat silent when his name was called and declined to participate in the fraud and folly. His contempt was further justified

---

21 See Calhoun's speeches and remarks in the Senate in *Calhoun Papers*, vol. 23, pp. 92–95, 98–103, 164–165, 172–173, 335–336; vol. 24, pp. 115–133, 195–210; and vol. 25, pp. 54–95, 235–254, 401 ff. Unless otherwise indicated, all quotations below come from these speeches.

when over 60 Whig members of Congress, who had voted for the war resolution because they were afraid of being labelled unpatriotic, immediately voted nay to appropriations to carry out the war.

The Constitution had been thrust aside: "a deed had been done from which the country would not be able to recover for a long time, if ever ... it has dropped a curtain between the present and the future" and "it has closed the first volume of our political history under the constitution, and opened the second ... no mortal could tell what would be written in it." To his closest confidante, his daughter Anna, Calhoun wrote: "Our people have undergone a great change. Their inclination is for conquest & empire, regardless of their institutions and liberty; or, rather, they think they hold their liberty by a divine tenure, which no imprudence, or folly on their part, can defeat."[22]

As the war successfully proceeded, Calhoun opposed the Polk administration's campaign to invade deep into Mexico, capture the capital, and force a government that would negotiate away territory. He spoke again and again for limited and justifiable war aims. The Rio Grande was secured. New Mexico and California, which had never been more than marginal parts of Mexico, were ours. Be content with this, he argued, when many voices were being raised for decisive defeat of Mexico and occupation of more of its territory. Calhoun went unheeded. Military success was gratifying and Polk invaded all the way to Mexico City and seized it, involving Americans for the first time in occupation of a foreign people.

What Calhoun had to say in the Senate:

> We have heard much of the reputation which our country has acquired by this war. I acknowledge it to the full amount, as far as the military is concerned. The army has done its duty nobly, and conferred high honours on the country, for which I sincerely thank them; but I apprehend that the reputation acquired does not go beyond this—and that, in other respects, we have lost

---

22 *Calhoun Papers*, vol. 25, p. 42.

rather than acquiring reputation by the war. It would seem certain, from all publications abroad, that the Government itself has not gained reputation in the eyes of the world for justice, moderation, or wisdom ... and in this view it appears that we have lost abroad, as much in civil and political reputation as we have acquired for our skill and valour in arms ....

Of the boundary to be drawn at the end of the war:

> ... it should be such as would deprive Mexico in the smallest possible degree of her resources and her strength; for, in aiming to do justice to ourselves in establishing the line, we ought, in my opinion, to inflict the least possible amount of injury on Mexico. I hold, indeed, that we ought to be just and liberal to her. Not only because she is our neighbour; not only because she is a sister republic; not only because she is emulous now, in the midst of all her difficulties, and has ever been, to imitate our example by establishing a federal republic; not only because she is one of the two great powers on this continent of all the States that have grown out of the provinces formerly belonging to Spain and Portugal—though these are high considerations, which every American ought to feel, and which every generous and sympathetic heart would feel, yet there are others which refer more immediately to ourselves. The course of policy which we ought to pursue in regard to Mexico is one of the greatest problems in our foreign relations. Our true policy, in my opinion, is, not to weaken or humble her; on the contrary, it is our interest to see her strong, and respectable, and capable of sustaining all the relations that ought to exist between independent nations. I hold that there is a mysterious connection between the fate of this country and that of Mexico; so much so, that her independence and capability of sustaining herself are almost as essential to our

prosperity, and the maintenance of our institutions, as they are to hers. Mexico is to us the forbidden fruit; the penalty of eating it would be to subject our institutions to political death.... When I said that there was a mysterious connection between the fate of our country and that of Mexico, I had reference to the great fact that we stood in such relation to her that we could make no disposition of Mexico, as a subject or conquered nation, that would not prove disastrous to us... you have looked into history and are too well acquainted with the fatal effects which large provincial possessions have ever had on the institutions of free states—to need any proof to satisfy you how hostile it would be to the institutions of this country, to hold Mexico as a subject province. There is not an example on record of any free state holding a province of the same extent and population, without disastrous consequences.

But before leaving this part of the subject, I must enter my solemn protest, as one of the representatives of a State of this Union, against pledging protection to any government established in Mexico under our countenance or encouragement. It would inevitably be overthrown as soon as our forces are withdrawn; and we would be compelled, in fulfilment of plighted faith, implied or expressed, to return and reinstate such Government in power, to be again overturned and again reinstated, until we should be compelled to take the government into our own hands, just as the English have been compelled to do again and again in Hindostan, under similar circumstances, until it has led to its entire conquest.

I must say I am at a loss to see how a free and independent republic can be established in Mexico under the protection and authority of its conquerors. I can readily understand how an aristocracy or a despotic government might be, but how a free republican government can be so established, under such circumstances, is to me incomprehensible. I had always supposed that such a government must be the spontaneous wish of the people; that it must emanate from the hearts of the people, and be supported by their devotion to it, without support from abroad. But it seems that these are antiquated notions—obsolete ideas—and that free popular governments may be made under the authority and protection of a conqueror.

We make a great mistake in supposing all people are capable of self-government. Acting under that impression, many are anxious to force free governments on all the peoples of this continent, and over the world, if they had the power. It has been lately urged in a very respectable quarter, that it is the mission of our country to spread civil and religious liberty over all the globe, and especially over this continent—even by force, if necessary. It is a sad delusion. None but a people advanced to a high state of moral and intellectual excellence are capable, in a civilised condition, of forming and maintaining free governments; and among those who are so advanced, very few indeed have had the good fortune to form constitutions capable of endurance .... It is harder to preserve than obtain liberty. After years of prosperity, the tenure by which it is held is too often forgotten; and, I fear, Senators, that such is the case with us. I have often been struck with the fact, that in the discussions of the great questions in which we are now engaged, relating to the origin and conduct of this war, the effect on free institutions and the liberty of the people have scarce been alluded to, although their bearing in that respect is so direct and disastrous .... But now, other topics occupy the attention of Congress and of the country—military glory, extension of the empire, and aggrandisement of the country.... We have had so many years of prosperity—passed through so many difficulties and dangers without the loss of liberty—that we begin to think we hold it by right divine from heaven itself. Under this impression, without thinking or reflecting, we plunge into war, contract heavy debts, increase vastly the patronage of the Executive, and indulge in every species of extravagance, without thinking that we expose our liberty to hazard. It is a great and fatal mistake. The day of retribution will come; and when it does, awful will be the reckoning, and heavy the responsibility somewhere.[23]

Calhoun did not believe in an American mission abroad and dreaded the consequences when so many of his fellow countrymen did. When the war was nearly concluded, Polk asked Congress for authorisation to occupy Yucatan, where the white population was being decimated by war with the Indians. He justified this on humanitarian grounds and by the Monroe Doctrine. The Doctrine was directed against imperialists from beyond the New World, Calhoun said. It had never been intended to justify U.S. intervention in other American countries. He knew whereof he spoke: he was the last surviving member of the Monroe Cabinet which had vetted the doctrine. But his statement, did not, of course, prevent American imperialists later in the century from claiming the contrary.

---

23 *Calhoun Papers*, vol. 25, pp. 401 — 404.

Calhoun and Slavery as a "Positive Good": What He Said

THE "POSITIVE GOOD" SPEECH of February 6, 1837, is vintage Calhoun, an exercise of his conception of the proper role of a statesmen placed in the highest deliberative body of the Union. That role was to look beyond the present clamour and clatter of routine politics and discern the deeper forces at work and what present choices and trends meant for the future.

As Andrew Lytle said in his essay on Calhoun, the role of a statesmen is to define clearly for a people the alternatives before them. This Calhoun sought to practice not only in regard to abolitionism, but with all big issues. This is why thoughtful people of the North as well as the South for forty years gave serious attention to what he had to say. This is why, alone among the American public figures of his time, he is still studied as a thinker.

There is no doubt that in 1837 he intended to change the political dynamic in regard to abolitionism. In keeping with his conception of his role as an independent and far-seeing public figure, he had in 1816 forced revision of the National Bank into something better than the original design. A few years previous he had done the same with the tariff, which was now coming down. He would do it again later this same year when he left the opposition and supported Van Buren on the Independent Treasury. And again in 1844 when he forced the Texas issue into the presidential campaign after the front-runners of both parties had colluded to keep it out of sight.

Before making his dramatic and definitive public stand against the new form that antislavery had taken, he had observed it for several years until he was sure that it had revealed itself fully. Even more than this new phenomenon itself, Calhoun was prompted by the evasive behaviour of the everyday politicians of North and South to the critical considerations it raised. The unvarying instinct of everyday politicians is to avoid hard issues. Majorities in Congress and the party press pretended to regard abolitionism as a temporary outbreak of enthusiasm which would soon die away as other such irrelevant, intemperate, and impossible enthusiasms had.

In the meantime, they claimed, it was best to pay as little attention to the abolitionists as possible except to throw them a scrap now and then to keep them quiet and avoid the appearance of disdaining such earnest if misguided citizens. Any Southerner who responded to them was immediately labeled by both political parties as an agitator and disunionist, stirring up things that were best left alone.

Calhoun chose the occasion to positively defend the institution of slavery as it then existed in the South because of a new enemy that needed to be clearly identified and checked. The time of that session of Congress and the previous one had been consumed for weeks by abolition petitions. These had literally flooded the Congress. An entire large room in the National Archives, which I have visited, is needed to contain them. There had been interminable wrangling in both houses about how to deal with this unprecedented situation. We should be clear that nobody, North or South, Democrat or Whig, except for a tiny minority led by John Quincy Adams, intended to respond to these petitions.

The main difference of opinion was the degree of non-action that the petitions were to receive. Calhoun favoured refusing to receive them, lest Congress seem to countenance the hateful abuse they contained and to assume jurisdiction that it did not have over the subject of slavery. The parliamentary expedients adopted are complicated, but essentially both houses decided that it was somehow better not to appear to deny the right of petition but to receive and immediately table them. This procedure did not prevent John Quincy Adams from proclaiming that a Southern slave power was choking out the sacred rights of northern citizens.

Calhoun wanted to hold up to public view the nature of this new movement and to confront what he regarded as the politicians' irresponsible avoidance of a grave issue. Knowing Calhoun as well as I do, his primary goal, I believe, was to convince the South that a lukewarm defense was no longer a proper stance. He began his address by calling for the Secretary to read two randomly selected petitions recently received by the Senate. Then he spoke:

> Such ... is the language held towards us and ours. The peculiar institutions of the South ... is pronounced to be sinful and odious, in the sight of God and man; and this with a systematic design of rendering us hateful in the eyes of the world, with a view to a general crusade against us and our institutions. This too, in the legislative halls of the Union, created by the confederated States, for the better protection of their peace, their safety, and their respective institutions; and yet we ... are expected to sit here in silence, hearing ourselves and our constituents day after day denounced ... if we but open our lips, the charge of agitation is resounded on all sides ... Every reflecting mind must see in this, a state of things deeply and dangerously diseased.

[A sidebar on the ongoing misuse of the term "peculiar institution." Calhoun did not mean that the institution was strange. He meant that it was peculiar to the Southern region as cod-fishing was peculiar to New England.]

He next made the point that abolitionism was not going to go away; unless called to account by vigorous rejection it would grow. He continued:

> However sound the great body of the non-slaveholding States are at present, in the course of a few years they will be succeeded by those who will have been taught to hate the people and institutions of nearly one half of the Union, with a hatred more deadly than one hostile nation ever entertained toward another. It is easy to see the end. By the necessary course of events ... we must become, finally, two peoples.

Such righteous revolutionary zeal would not fade away but would use every small victory as a base for a further attack until finally the South would have to surrender or to separate and defend itself. Because the North had adopted a false constitutional theory that the federal government was the judge of its own limits, the abolitionists believed that they had the responsibility and the power to reconstruct Southern society. Rising generations of Northerners would be fed on relentless defamation of the South. The ranks of the abolitionists would increase until they formed a block large enough that Northern politicians would compete for their votes. As he said, "there are kind feelings towards us on the part of the great body of the non-slaveholding States, but as kind as their feelings may be, we may rest assured that no political party in those States will risk their ascendancy for our safety."

The Union and abolition could not co-exist, he said. The Union was in danger. Here Calhoun was not far from what Jefferson said in his fire-bell letter: "A geographical line, coinciding with a marked principle, moral and political, once conceived and held up to the angry passions of men, will never be obliterated; and every new irritation will mark it deeper and deeper." To assert that the Union and abolition could not co-exist was unwelcome, but it was true. As always, Calhoun was acting the statesman, discerning what the present foretold of the future.

With this introduction Calhoun was ready to reply to the abolitionist attack on the South, and to do so he had to discuss the realities of Southern life as he and his colleagues knew them. According to the abolitionists the South was a land of horrors devoid of religion and decency and law and order, inhabited by depraved white barbarians and black people out of whom all humanity had been crushed. Calhoun and all Southerners knew this to be a false picture. Neither the whites nor the blacks of the South resembled their portraits as painted by the abolitionists.

Mr. Calhoun "insisted that the slaveholders of the South had nothing in the case to lament or to lay to their conscience .... Nor was there anything in the doctrines he held in the slightest degree inconsistent with the highest and purest principles of freedom. Be it good or bad, it has grown up with our society and institutions .... But let me not be understood as admitting even by implication that the existing relations between the two races in the slaveholding States is an evil—far otherwise; I hold it to be a good, as it has thus far proved itself to be to both and will continue to prove so if not disturbed by the fell spirit of abolition."

Never before in history, he continued, has the black race "attained a condition so civilised and so improved, not only physically but morally and intellectually ... in the course of a few generations it has grown up under the fostering care of our institutions, as reviled as they have been, to its present comparative civilised condition." The rapid increase of numbers, nearly equal to the white population, Calhoun, said "is conclusive proof" of the advancement and of the relative comfort of this class of Southern labourers.

Nor had the white race degenerated. "... I appeal to all sides whether the South is not equal in virtue, intelligence, patriotism, courage, disinterestedness, and all the high qualities which adorn our nature. I ask whether we have not contributed our full share of talents and political wisdom in forming and sustaining this political fabric; and whether we have not constantly inclined most strongly to the side of liberty and been the first to see and first to resist the encroachments of power. In one thing only are we inferior—the arts of gain ...." Further:

> I hold that in the present state of civilisation, where two races of different origin are brought together, the relation now existing in the slaveholding States between the two, is, instead of an evil, a good—a positive good. I feel myself called upon to speak freely upon the subject where the honour and interests of those I represent are involved.

Calhoun's description of Southern society was not eccentric or new. Episcopal Bishop John Henry Hopkins of Vermont was to declare: "The South has done more than any people on earth for the African race."

Many Southerners were ready for Calhoun's message. Most educated Southerners had read about and some had seen the degraded and hopeless poor of New York and London. They knew that women and children in New York were working 16 hour days for starvation wages. A few years later it was reliably reported that there were in the city 150,000 unemployed and 40,000 homeless. As well as 600 brothels and 9,000 grog shops where the poor could drown their sorrows. There was little reason for the planter to wallow in guilt.

Our visceral distaste for whatever is connected with the word "slavery," tends to disguise for us the enormity of what the abolitionists demanded. We imagine that the South was resisting a humane and reasonable proposition to give up its evil ways. Northerners were zealous to squeeze every possible penny of personal profit out of government policy, yet were proposing that the South literally perform the vastest act of self-disinheritance in history, and launch its society into a revolutionary gamble that would alter the life of every person and could well bring disaster and destroy the hopes of its posterity. In the 21st century it is easily to overlook that the African-American population was a majority in three Southern states and in a vast swath of territory from Southside Virginia to East Texas, while in Massachusetts it was around 1 per cent.

We are now so used to demands for revolutionary alteration of society in the pursuit of virtue, such an inclination is so firmly a part of the American national business, that it is hard to comprehend the situation presented. This demand upon Southerners came from people who were obviously hostile and who assumed a power that was not theirs to demand a revolution for which they bore no direct responsibility and from the consequences of which they would not suffer. This in a Union which Southern fathers and grandfathers had established to make secure the welfare of their sons and grandsons. A Union which they had contributed more than their fair share to build and sustain and upon which they had made no selfish demands. As Calhoun said on a later occasion: "When did the South ever lay its hand upon the North?"

In our present society it is thought that good people are those who submit to being reconstructed in the cause of virtue. The people who were thus addressed belonged to another tradition. They believed in personal responsibility for exercise of their rights and duties and in the necessity of guarding against potential infringements upon their freedom of action. Otherwise, they would not have been the kind of men who conquered a continental wilderness and founded free institutions.

There were no precedents for emancipation on such a scale. The few precedents that existed were unencouraging. There was Haiti; and in the British West Indies, the small population of slave owners had been compensated and gone back home while the islands, once the most valuable in the world, had sunk into poverty.

Abolitionists vigorously rejected compensation to slave owners; it would be rewarding sinners. Even at minimum it was beyond what was a conceivable public expenditure. Although, as has been pointed out, it would have been cheaper than the cost of the war. The difference is that the North enjoyed the profits of the war, while only the South would have profited from compensated emancipation.

Colonization had failed, though it would continue to be held up as a solution, mostly notably by Abraham Lincoln. The Virginia constitutional convention in the shadow of the Nat Turner massacre of white children had despaired of any remedy except for the South to keep on and to keep the matter in the hands of those involved.

Slavery was not confined to a few large plantations, contrary to propaganda. The plantation itself was not an obscene and accidental blot upon America. It was a far older and more fundamental part of life than the Union. About a fourth of the white families across the South had some stake in slavery, a far greater percentage than of the Northern people who owned stock in banks and tariff protected industries. Most of these slaveholdings were small—one or two families who lived and worked closely with their owners and moved with them in the pioneer stream westward to new lands. Slavery was not a proposition to be voted up or down—it was the warp and woof of everyday life in an area larger than Western Europe. It was a basic social institution and a vast distribution of private property, the future elimination of which would be the largest confiscation in history. And it was an inextricable part of the production of the exports that made international trade possible for Americans.

It is a common now to equate the Old South with Nazi Germany. Nothing proves more conclusively the historical ignorance and ideologically driven deceitfulness of present commentators. Servitude in the Old South was domestic—people were held to labour by families, not by a totalitarian state. Such servitude is a vastly familiar in human history. There was no barbed wire around the plantations, hardly anything that could even be called a police force in the South. True, the legal theory of chattel slavery was harsh, though not as harsh as has been represented. But the plantations were homes and farms where people were born, lived, and buried, not arbitrary and lawless but governed by longstanding custom and public opinion, the immemorial rounds of agriculture, and the give and take of everyday life. Far from being seats of hopeless barbarity, they were the homes and livelihoods of more than half of the great founders and early leaders of the United States. Many Northern and European visitors found them to be places of peace and contented life. Many of the survivors of plantation servitude interviewed in the 1930s remembered them as marked by a consoling and comfortable life—too many to be easily dismissed.

Disconnection from culture has proceeded so far that Americans are literally unable to imagine the past or understand any society except in terms of their own narrow reality. They cannot conceive of a society that was familial but not egalitarian. This destroys the capacity to understand not only Old South but the Bible and most of history and the world's great literature.

If one wants to bring up fascism, it was the North which invaded, occupied, and seized the wealth of other people's lands and did so without apology and glorying in the right of the stronger to dispose of the weaker. Often before and during the war Northern leaders vaunted their pure Anglo-Saxonism as superior to the inferior, mongrel breed of Southerners It was Hitler who admired Abraham Lincoln for ruthlessly crushing resistance to the central state.

The most fundamental obstacle the abolitionists did not address at all. What would happen to the black people turned out to fend for themselves? As free men they were almost universally regarded as inferior and unwelcome members of society, a situation in which the North was as complicit as the South, if not more so. And while the abolitionists were raging against the planters for abominable cruelty to their dependents, the more hard-nosed variety of Yankee was condemning them as bad, inefficient businessmen for being too good to the folks on the plantation and not extracting greater profit from their workers.

Slavery could not disappear for the simple reason that Americans were overwhelmingly opposed to citizenship and equality for black people and there was therefore no real alternative to the existing arrangement. Calhoun was accepting this fact realistically and concluding that the existing way was the best possible under the circumstances and that therefore Southern society embodied a good. Southerners had no reason to apologize.

We should recall that Abraham Lincoln on the eve of The War told the Northern public that "the Southern people are exactly what we would be in their situation." And, he said, even given unlimited power he would not know what to do about the existing slavery.

Calhoun proposed a reasonable answer, the only possible one and one that Southerners were already carrying out every day. To make the best of the situation into which they had been born, bringing to bear their good will, Christianity, and conscientious care for dependents. These were qualities which, of course, the abolitionists in their ignorance and malice denied that they possessed.

It was not all that unprecedented to refute attacks by challenging the portrayal of slavery as an evil. Calhoun deliberately, I think, emphasized the point by using the word "positive" along with "good." Even so, this speech would probably have passed into history with no more notice than many others if Calhoun had stopped with "positive good." Instead, as was his custom, he concluded by taking the higher ground of a philosophical view. He chose to take the war into enemy country, which is what, I suspect, really bothers those who declaimed against him then and now.

"I hold," he told the Senate and the country, "... that there never has yet existed a wealthy and civilised society in which one portion of the community did not ... live on the labour of the other." This was as true of the North as of the South. A conflict of interest and an uneven distribution of wealth marked all societies at all times. The South was trying one way to cope with this truth. Calhoun was not asking to stop the clock to defend a static institution to be kept forever behind a defensive bunker. Rather, he said, the South was engaged in an "experiment" which he believed had, all things considered, showed itself a good. The North was engaged in a different experiment. He was not yet willing to concede that the Southern way was inferior in the production of human happiness. Another decade, he suggested, would allow a better comparison.

Here Calhoun hardly differed from Massachusetts Founding Father John Adams. At the time of the Missouri controversy Adams told Jefferson that the slavery question was only a conflict over words and that he was perfectly willing to leave the issue to Southern men. He said that "in some countries the labouring poor were called freemen in others they were called slaves; but that the difference as to the state was imaginary only... That the condition of the labouring poor in most countries, that of the fishermen particularly in the Northern States, is as abject as that of slaves."

It is pretty evident from the commentary in Congress and the press, that what really bothered the critics of his famous speech was his insistence that the conflict of capital and labour was not a particular curse of the South. He refused to accept the scenario of Northern good and Southern evil.

In regard to the society of the Old South, Calhoun was more nearly right and the abolitionists more nearly wrong. In regard to the future he excelled all others in perception.

The position of African-Americans in the United States has long presented a moral challenge. But it is an evasion when thorny problems of the day receive a pseudo-solution by projection of blame onto the long dead slave owners of the Old South and their spokesmen. Unfortunately, this is a familiar habit for Americans.

Paper presented at Abbeville Institute Conference in the Rotunda, University of Virginia, 2010.

JOHN C. CALHOUN AND SLAVERY AS A "POSITIVE GOOD": WHAT CALHOUN *DID NOT* SAY

IN WHAT BECAME THE UNITED STATES, servitude of people of the black African race existed for about two and a half centuries. The subject of American slavery is today so entertwined with unhealthy and present-centered emotions and motives—guilt, shame, hypocrisy, projection, prurient imagination, propaganda, vengeance, extortion—as to defy rational historical discussion. Curiously, the much longer flourishing of African bondage—in the Caribbean and South America, in Africa itself, and in the Muslim world—seldom enters into American consciousness.

It is appropriate therefore to commence the understanding of this critical part of American history with an investigation of the antislavery movement. There will come a time, perhaps, when it will be necessary and possible to examine American slavery itself in order to appreciate fully what Calhoun meant when, in a speech in the Senate on February 6, 1837, he used the words "positive good" to describe the long-established institution of domestic slavery in his Southern society.

In undertaking to put Calhoun in the right context I will try to succinctly describe the abolitionist movement that arose in the 1830s, which was the cause and immediate occasion for Calhoun's famous statement. Prior to the outbreak of the new abolitionism, antislavery sentiment had been widespread. Slavery's economic and political defects, real and imagined, were freely discussed and gentle Quakers went about the business of promoting individual emancipation. Indeed, in the early 19th century one of my North Carolina ancestors freed his few slaves as a matter of conscience.

It was Calhoun's purpose to call attention to the changed nature of antislavery and what that meant for the American future. To make a long story short, this new antislavery campaign was a crusade of evangelistic Christian heresy bent on purging the world of other people's sins. It repudiated friendly persuasion and preached hatred of the slave-owner, indeed of all Southern society, in truly vile terms of abuse. According to the new abolitionism of the 1830s in sermons, press, and voluminous petitions to Congress, the South was a House of Horror inhabited by depraved whites and tortured blacks. Slavery was a sin to be purged immediately and without any attention to practical details.

A lurid imaginary conception of slavery rather than the everyday reality of life in the South, about which most knew nothing, energized the abolitionists. Little attention was paid to the actual welfare and future of the black people, who appear mostly as suffering victims in a melodrama and humble recipients of Northern benevolence. It is often difficult to tell whether the abolitionists most feared slavery or the presence of black people. By the late antebellum period, New England's premier intellectual, Waldo Emerson, was predicting approvingly that the blacks, when free and deprived of the paternal care of the Southern whites they had irreparably corrupted, would soon die away and be as extinct as the dodo, leaving America to the pure Anglo-Saxon.

In the context we should make clear that the fanatical temper of this new mass movement alarmed not only Southerners but most of the orthodox Christian clergy and the general citizenry of the North. Also, that it was not a North-wide phenomenon, but was centered in areas settled by the poorer class of New Englanders. These regions, especially Vermont, western New York, and parts of the Midwest, were widely recognised as the source of other strange "isms" as well as abolition—of Mormonism, Seventh Day Adventism, spiritualism, prohibitionism, Anti-Masonism, vegetarianism, feminism, and free-love-ism among others. The outbreak of reformist zeal had more to do with the internal religious and social tensions and the breakdown of Calvinist orthodoxy within this specific greater New England culture region than with Southern realities. The tensions and unrest were projected outward, in honoured puritan fashion, towards the sins of others. This same region furnished John Brown with the financial backers and accomplices for his expeditions. A lower class phenomenon, this zeal yet comported well in its thrust with the Transcendentalism that was attracting New England intellectuals.

One could make several large books just studying the Northern condemnation of what was deemed the fanatical and meddling spirit of New Englanders. A prominent New York Democratic writer said:

> The Abolitionists have throughout committed the fatal mistake of urging a purely moral cause by means, not only foreign to that character, but hostile to it, incompatible with it. Where they had to persuade, they have undertaken to force. Where love was the spirit in which they should have approached the task, they have done it in that of hate.

It becomes evident to anyone on close examination, although Calhoun did not mention this aspect, that abolitionist propaganda was a form of pornography, dwelling on the possibilities of sexual license in the master/slave relationship. The great abolitionist preacher Henry Ward Beecher, brother of Mrs. Stowe of "Uncle Tom's Cabin" fame, made money by selling tickets to pretend slave auctions featuring young, almost-white women for sale, while preying on the young wives of his own congregation.

The abolitionist mindset has long dominated American history and absorbed Calhoun's defense of slavery into its own telling of the American story. A common, widely accepted history of American antislavery goes something like this:

Negro slavery was an unfortunate relic of colonialism. Our all-wise Founding Fathers, including the great statesmen from the South, intended to put it on the road to extinction. After all, in 1776 they declared to the world that "All Men Are Created Equal," in 1785 they banned slaves from the vast unsettled territory North and West of the Ohio River, and they continued thereafter to speak of slavery as undesirable. In this account it is not always mentioned that opposition to slavery was mostly theoretical and was usually linked with impractical notions about the removal of the emancipated blacks from the midst of American society.

Then, according to the conventional account, something terrible happened that changed the course of history. The cotton gin made slavery once more profitable. Southerners, through their greed (from which Northerners seem to have been free), reversed the intentions of the Founders and begin to cling to and defend their awful institution from the criticism of benevolent, enlightened, and progressive Northerners. If not for this unfortunate invention, slavery would have dwindled away.

Then, in 1832 South Carolina, driven to treason by its hysterical devotion to slavery, invented States rights and nullified the tariff. This action was illegal, unconstitutional, unprecedented, based entirely on a fraudulent version of the Constitution, intended to break up the Union, and was a blow struck at the prosperity and progress of all true Americans.

But, as the story goes, this was only the prelude to a long treasonous conspiracy of the "Slave Power." The Slave Power was imagined as a ruthless, violent class of large slave-holders who kept the blacks and most of the whites of the South in ignorance, poverty, and subjection, imperiously and selfishly ruled the Union, and in its arrogance even designed to spread slavery to the virtuous North. It was the implacable enemy of Northern rights and American values.

The Slave Power conspiracy took a decisive step forward in 1837, when the evil genius John C. Calhoun of South Carolina, in another turning point in history, declared that slavery was not an unfortunate evil but a desirable thing, a "positive good." Calhoun, of course, was motivated by bitter spite from having been thwarted in his insatiable ambition to become President. Thereafter, he and his disciples laboured unceasingly to spread the scourge of slavery and to rule or ruin the United States.

SLAVERY AS A "POSITIVE GOOD": WHAT CALHOUN DID NOT SAY

The conspiracy of the slave-holding elite reached its height with secession. In its wickedness and folly the Slave Power sought to destroy government of, by, and for the people. Southerners engaged in rebellion against the best government on earth and rejected the saintly Lincoln, who had been chosen by the people and by God to lead the country through its greatest crisis. Only those perverted by slavery could have made such a diabolical attempt to destroy the United States, the last best hope of mankind.

Inevitably, the wicked rebellion instigated by the Slave Power was defeated by the forces of righteousness, and the Great Emancipator, in the noblest act in history, struck the chains from enslaved black people and made them forever free, something which he had longed for piously from his youth. The earlier version of the tale featured adoring blacks at the feet of noble emancipators like Lincoln and Robert Gould Shaw. A revised version pictures noble self-emancipated blacks and noble boys in blue rushing into each other's arms to overthrow the brutal Southern masters. Neither version gives a remotely truthful perspective on what actually happened during the catastrophic bloodletting of 1861-1865.

This scenario is widely believed and may be the interpretation of the Civil War era held by the largest number of Americans. As an account of American history it is false in every particular. It is a fairy tale made up to sustain the notion that America, except for the South, is uniquely virtuous among the nations and always motivated by high and benevolent ideals. It covers with righteousness and inevitability the brutal war of conquest, domination, and exploitation that was waged against the Southern people from 1861 to 1876. It is the rehashed propaganda of one side in a vast and complex conflict, not the sober judgment of history. We feel its power when George W. Bush talks about an American mission to spread virtue throughout the world, no matter how many ungrateful people have to be killed. He is heir to the abolitionist playbook which tells us that America, democracy, and Christianity are endowed with a mission to purify the world of evil.

This was the predominant mode of telling American history before the 20th century, though in published works it appeared in a more circumstantial and sophisticated form. In order to understand the propagandistic misrepresentation of Calhoun we need to see where the fairy tale fudges the truth.

In the first half of the 20th century the evil South interpretation of the Civil War was questioned and altered to a considerable extent by professional historians who were trained to examine primary sources exhaustively and skeptically. Their inclination was to look at both sides of a controversy in search of a larger truth rather than view the past as a story of good guys and bad guys. These historians were also disillusioned by the moralistic righteousness that had justified the catastrophic and fruitless death toll of the Great War. Further, they were willing, while unsympathetic to the South, to perceive the self-interest that marked the North in the sectional controversy. And were not persuaded that the Big Business empire created by the Northern victory was altogether a wonderful thing.

The premier American historian, Charles A. Beard, wrote that the Civil War was was not a civil war and not about slavery, but was a clash between the ruling classes of two regions with competing economic interests. Other historians were not afraid to describe the irrational nature of abolitionism and to discover that opposition to slavery was not necessarily motivated by benevolence toward the slave. And some historians saw the conflict not as inevitable but as resulting from extremism and blunders by political leaders of both sides that brought about a crisis that no sensible person wanted. As one scholar has put it, The War was about "an imaginary Negro in an impossible place."

In our time the fairy tale interpretation of The War has come back with a vengeance. It is reflected in the much hyped TV series by Ken Burns and in the most sophisticated and celebrated histories of the day. There is not time to go into the interesting question of why this is so, but, despite claims to the contrary, it has absolutely nothing to do with actual historical knowledge and expertise having reached a higher truth. Having engaged in a good many arguments over the years, I have realised that the propagators of this view are often guilty of extreme lack of actual knowledge about the events and conditions of 19th century America. I know of a graduate student who in a paper mentioned Jefferson's and Madison's strong allegiance to state rights. A tenured full professor of American history told the student that he had made it up—it couldn't be true. This "scholar" knew what he had been taught, that State rights was something invented out of the air by John C. Calhoun in the cause of slavery. Much of the present insistence that an evil Southern defense of slavery is the complete explanation for the war of 1861–1865 rests on this kind of ignorant adherence to fashionable dogma.

The fairy tale now takes the form of a hardened Cultural Marxist party line. Revolutionary change is always good and those who oppose it always evil. The only significance of the war is that it was a destruction of the Southern ruling class through the ongoing dialectic of revolution. The only thing to be regretted is that more recalcitrant Southerners were not killed and even greater revolutionary change was not forced upon American society. Differing interpretations are heresies to be suppressed, not arguments to be answered. They are damned as "revisionism." Revisionism used to mean simply a revised historical interpretation, something harmless that occurred naturally every once in a while. It is now a term of abuse meant to suggest that objectors to the official interpretation of the Civil War are in the same company as those "revisionists" who deny Nazi atrocities in World War II.

Honest historians understand that they have their own sympathies, values, and assumptions, and try to allow for their own bias in interpreting the past. Advocates of the present orthodoxy do not qualify as honest historians. The orthodoxy is believable only from the starting point of a number of unacknowledged and unexamined beliefs: The assumptions are so much a part of the mental equipment of contemporary intellectuals that they are not even aware of them. Assumptions:

> *That one need pay no attention to any Southern viewpoint because Southern words were always and only rationalizations for evil deeds and motives.

*That one need not examine the motives, agenda, and behaviour of abolitionism because it was the instrument of revolution, resistance to which is always justly exterminated.

*That Southerners had no culture of their own, no distinct identity, no worthy qualities, not even any intelligent grasp of their own economic interests—nothing to sustain a right to independence except devotion to slavery. Deeply underlying these unrecognised assumptions is another—Southerners do not really count as Americans and are a disposable people.

When Calhoun rose in the Senate in 1837 he was not launching a pro-slavery conspiracy—he was taking an open and defensive stance against a new and extreme provocation.

He was not declaring that slavery in the abstract was always and everywhere a good thing—he took pains to make clear that he was talking about the existing American society, about a specific historical situation and not a theory. In the discussion that followed his speech Calhoun "denied having pronounced slavery in the abstract a good. All he had said of it referred to existing circumstances …."

He was not throwing up a roadblock to the progress of emancipation because slavery was not dwindling away before he spoke. The most obvious proof that there was no serious possibility of abolishing slavery is that it was flourishing. It was not as large in American life as it had been in the 18th century, but the slaves had increased vastly in number and spread over an immense territory in company with the white population. At no time was slavery economically moribund, though some times were better than others. The economic stagnation that had marked the older South was being overcome by agricultural reform.

True, there had been some quiet progress in individual emancipation. There were more free black people in the slave States than in the free, and they were more prosperous and had a better place in society than in the North. Both Southern and European visitors to the North testified to the depressed and despised condition of the latter. Another of those many facts about the antebellum South that our fairy tale history never mentions. The great man of the North,

Daniel Webster, was to point out in the debates over the Compromise of 1850, that it was not Southern spokesmen but the fanaticism of the abolitionists that destroyed the disposition toward emancipation that had flourished before they appeared.

Calhoun was most certainly not acting out of personal ambition or a desire to rule or ruin the Union. A brilliant and experienced man, he understood the operation of the American political system as well as anyone ever has. Thus he knew perfectly well by this time that no statesman could ever again be elected President. He kept his name in play for the Presidency because it lent greater attention to what he had to say. As he said on another occasion, certain politicians were always attributing political stands to personal motives because they were unable themselves to conceive of any motives that were not personal.

And Calhoun was not launching some great innovation in the Southern attitude toward slavery because most of what he had to say was already a well-developed part of American discourse.

Calhoun's speech of 1837 could be characterised as an aggressive and innovative repudiation of previous American doctrine only in the light of the fairy tale history that there had been a commitment to emancipation at the Founding. The misrepresentation of this occasion was deliberate and malicious propaganda that reveals much about the nature of antislavery.

It is still today vigorously asserted that the Founding Fathers contemplated the elimination of slavery, although somehow they did not quite get around to it. Though many of the founding generation regretted the existence of slavery, it is absurd to say that they contemplated a decree of emancipation. It has been pointed out that the Constitution explicitly recognised the existence of slavery in several ways, but that is not the main point that can be made. The idea of some firm but deferred commitment to end slavery rests upon the completely anachronistic assumption that the framers of the Constitution were omnipotent and omniscient sages who were free to design a New World Order out of their divine wisdom. This is a reflection of the nationalist fantasy history that was developing at the same time and in tandem with abolitionism. The Framers not only never had an intention to interfere with the slavery that existed, they would never have dreamed that they had any power to do so. The Constitution was an agreement among the states to preserve their existing societies.

Slavery was not dwindling away on the eve of the American Revolution. The slave population was growing, mostly naturally in pace with the American population in general. In fact, slave ownership was actually increasing in some of the Northern colonies. The two great Revolutionary heroes of Massachusetts, John Hancock and Samuel Adams, were slave-owners who brought their dependants with them to the Continental councils in Philadelphia.

The Northwest Ordinance of 1785, banning slaves from the land north and west of the Ohio river, is portrayed as a conclusive avowal of antislavery determination among the Founders. It was nothing of the sort. Since in the Continental Congress each state had one vote, it more resembles an agreement among the states to divide territory, like the later Missouri Compromise, than a popular determination to advance emancipation. In 1785 the importation of more slaves from Africa was still open and, as far as anyone knew, would remain so indefinitely. If the geography of slavery were not limited, the country could fill up with more black population, which nobody wanted. The natural increase of the slave population was already abundant. Among other things, additional imports to fill up all the unsettled territory of the Union would decrease the value of slave property in the East. So little binding was the territorial restriction on the future of slavery in the Old Northwest that the Illinois legislature not long after statehood gravely considered a proposal to make slavery legal in its borders.

By the time of the Missouri controversy of 1819 – 1820, the situation had changed greatly. Foreign importations were illegal by general consent. The Jeffersonian leadership unequivocally repudiated the attempted restriction on slavery in Missouri and the territories. The retired statesmen Jefferson and Madison agreed that the restriction on Missouri was unconstitutional, was a cynical political maneuver by Federalists to divide Northern and Southern Republicans and achieve rule, and that the extension of slavery was a phony issue. They said so repeatedly and emphatically in their letters. Jefferson even used the term "so-called" to refer to the extension of slavery issue. Forbidding the so-called "extension" of slavery did not free a single slave and in fact retarded gradual emancipation.

It is true that these gentlemen, though by no means all Southern leaders, had previously expressed a desire to be rid of slavery, if that were possible, and that they continued to do so. But in 1819–1820 they also vigorously denied the right of the Northern majority in Congress to interfere with slavery. The antislavery that had appeared in the Missouri issue they regarded as illegal, unwise, inexpedient, hypocritical, and portentous of disaster. This is what Jefferson meant when he referred at the time to "the fire bell in the night." The terror that awakened him was not slavery but the dangerous portent of antislavery.

At the same time Nathaniel Macon of North Carolina, William Smith of South Carolina, and other members of Congress denied that slavery in the South was "barbaric" and defended it as a paternalistic good. John Taylor made the same case in his *Inquiry*, which he was provoked to publish by the Missouri question. The most solid Jeffersonians of the North tended to agree.

In 1830, seven years before Calhoun uttered "positive good," Robert Y. Hayne of South Carolina had this to say during his celebrated debates with Webster:

> Sir, when arraigned before the bar of public opinion on this charge of slavery, we can stand up with conscious rectitude, plead not guilty, and put ourselves upon God and our country. If slavery, as it now exists in this country, be an evil, we of the present found it ready made to our hands. Finding our lot cast among a people, whom God had manifestly committed to our care, we did not sit down to speculate on abstract questions of theoretical liberty. We met it as a practical question of obligation and duty. We resolved to make the best of the situation in which Providence had placed us, and to fulfill the high trust which had devolved upon us as the

owners of slaves, in the only way in which such a trust could be fulfilled without spreading misery and ruin throughout the land.

When in the 1850s a Northern party formed around opposition to the so-called "extention" of slavery, it laid a thoroughly dishonest claim on the name Republican and the heritage of Jefferson. Exclusion of slavery from the territories was portrayed as the Jeffersonian policy and used as a front by a mercantilist party that represented the extreme opposite of all that Jeffersonian Republicanism had stood for. So remote had the Northern understanding of the American past become that a party which existed to force through every policy that Jefferson despised, claimed him. Southerners still understood the Revolution and the Founding in intimate terms. They knew what their fathers and grandfathers had thought. In the North, American history had already become an abstraction, a matter of words to be cherry-picked for ammunition. This itself is an important story but far too large for this occasion. Along with tariff promoters declarations that Southern opposition to their profits was treasonous, the abolitionists embodied an attitude that Southerners were not fellow citizens but subjects whose lives and property existed for Northern benefit.

The conventional accounts of antislavery tend to ignore or justify the extremist, hateful, and obviously counter-productive rhetoric that denounced Southerners as enemies, tyrants, pirates, and kidnappers and the South as an alien abomination which must be purged from America. Even less noticed is the economic critique of the South that was flourishing at the same time in the calculations of the most hard-nosed Northern capitalists, who would eventually join with the abolitionists in the Republican Party. While the abolitionists were raging against the planters for abominable cruelty to their dependents, the capitalists were faulting them for being bad businessmen, too good to the workers on the plantation and failing to extract the maximum profit from them.

The belief was strong among them that slave labour was unwilling and therefore inefficient, though this theory was somewhat belied by the fact that the immense production of Southern tobacco in the

18th century and Southern cotton in the 19th century made up the overwhelming bulk of American exports. The capitalists and their spokesmen also believed and frequently said that slave labour was more expensive because it required the lifetime support of the worker. Something which for Southerners was a source of pride was seen by Northerners as a foolish waste of profits. If the workers were free to compete for wages, it was thought, productivity would be up and labour costs down. Often, this notion was accompanied by a belief that if lazy Southern blacks and whites could be got rid of and Southern lands settled by industrious New Englanders or Europeans, the profits of cotton would be all the greater and flowing into the pockets of people who really deserved them.

It seems to be the judgment of respected economic historians that the plantation was indeed a highly productive agricultural enterprise. Also, as Calhoun asserted in his "positive good" speech, that the black bondsmen received a greater lifetime return on their labour than industrial workers of the time in the North and Europe. Even before the end of the war and Reconstruction, opportunists followed the Union armies into the South, grabbed land, and set about to get rich with "free labour." It usually did not work. The Northern capitalist conception of Southern society was as misguided as the abolitionist. This powerful part of antislavery should be kept in mind when we hear Lincoln singing the praises of "free labour."

A planter might well have maximized return on his capital if he could somehow dispose of his land and slaves and invest like rich Northerners in government bonds and the stock of tariff-protected industries. But how could he possibly do this? And if he did so, what was to become of his people and his inherited way of life?

All of this was in Calhoun's understanding of his world when he rose to speak.

Paper presented at Abbeville Institute Conference in the Rotunda, University of Virginia, 2010

Cincinnatus, Call the Office!

THE UNITED STATES SENATE, one summer morning near the end of the session in 1842, was busy with routine reception of committee reports. The Committee on the Judiciary reported favorably on a bill to pay the estate of William Hull, whose heirs had petitioned for compensation for his government service. Hull had held appointments as General in command of the Northwest and as Governor of Michigan Territory at the beginning of the War of 1812.

Mr. Calhoun of South Carolina shattered the quiet routine of the Senate. He rose to express amazement at what he had just heard:

> He was, in the first place, surprised that the representatives of General Hull could ever think of presenting this claim to Congress. He would not be more so, if the representatives of [Benedict] Arnold should present a claim for his pay as a general in our service, after he had committed his treason, on the ground that he had held the commission of a general, which had not been revoked.

The deep and universal public condemnation of General Hull had never been reversed and never would be, Calhoun said. It was a matter Calhoun knew well, having at the time been a member of the House of Representatives straining desperately to support the war effort: Hull had surrendered his troops and the Detroit fortifications on the first appearance of the British, without firing a shot in resistance. He had blamed his act on the lack of preparation and support by his superiors—something which might excuse defeat but could not excuse cowardice. Hull was court-martialed and ordered to be shot, though President Madison had granted a reprieve.

Calhoun asked the Senate:

> How could his pay as Governor be allowed, when there was, for the time, no such Territory as Michigan? It had, by his own act, become a British Province and remained so till it was re-conquered by the army under General Harrison. With what show, then, of justice or equity, could he be paid for governing a territory that did not exist, and which had ceased to exist by his own act? The error of the committee consisted in supposing that the commission—the mere paper and wax—and not the service, gave the pay.

What a contrast, Calhoun continued, this situation presented with the conduct of General Andrew Jackson. A federal judge had fined Jackson $1,000 for supposed damages to certain private property in preparing the defenses of New Orleans. Jackson had paid the fine from his own pocket and got on with the business of winning the battle and concluding the war with a great victory. Yet Jackson had never been compensated. "How strange that such unequal justice should be meted out by the committee to General Jackson, who terminated the war with glory, and General Hull, who commenced it with disgrace!"

Calhoun might well have expanded his examples from the history of American republican virtue. George Washington had stood in the Continental Congress in 1775 and acknowledged his acceptance of the perilous mission of taking command of the Continental forces already engaged in fighting with the world's greatest power. He would accept no pay, Washington said, though he hoped that the Congress would repay his expenses in their service. And at the end of the war, Washington, like the Roman hero Cincinnatus, had disbanded his army and returned to his private life, even though there was plenty of room for dissatisfaction at niggling and inadequate response to his claims.

General Hull's bill, among other things, demonstrates the difference between Southerners and people from lower New England. Hull was, not surprisingly, from Connecticut, which has supplied a vastly disproportionate share of bad examples in American history:

Benedict Arnold, P.T. Barnum, John Brown, William O. Douglas, William F. Buckley, Lowell Weicker, the Bush family, etc. Senator Calhoun, a former Secretary of War, was well aware that Massachusetts and Connecticut had more men receiving Revolutionary War pensions than they had ever had active soldiers, while Francis Marion's veterans and the heroes of Kings Mountain, who had played a vital part in winning American independence, had never considered patriotism as a claim on the Treasury, but even if they had would lack the proper paperwork. Everyone was aware that Massachusetts had for a quarter century been presenting annually a demand to Congress to be paid for the non-service of its militia in the War of 1812.

The incident of the bill to compensate the Hull heirs illustrates a late phase of the struggle in the American polity between office as an honour and a trust and office as a source of profit. Virtue was obviously already on the defensive in Calhoun's day, though the Founding generation had had a strong sense that the diminishing of virtue would spell doom for the noble experiment of self-government of the people. Though the need for virtue in the people and in their leaders was a given, the exact connotations of the concept could differ. From the beginning, the New England idea of republican virtue had a commercial, collectivist, government-as-engine-of-prosperity cast which harked back to the Puritan Commonwealth. The more idealistic version below the Susquehanna drew on an idea of the highest patriotism of republican Rome. (Whether the idea was historically accurate or not is another question.) It was no accident that Addison's "Cato" was Washington's favorite play and that he was often depicted in Roman garb, that officers of the War of Independence called their veterans group the Society of the Cincinnati, and that the seats of the American governments were called capitols. Indeed, Thomas Jefferson modeled the capitol of Virginia on a Roman building he had seen in France.

The idea was this: that to lead the people was an obligation, an honor and a trust, which, properly executed, was the highest example of patriotism and the most worthy of fame. Office should not be a job, a source of profit, or an opportunity for self-promotion. Ambition for glory could be excused as the engine of patriotic effort, but ambition for money and power was defection from republican virtue and signaled a taste for usurpation and corruption. Difficult as it may be to believe today, in the early Republic public office often required a sacrifice of private interests. Many good men found that after one duty-dictated term in the House, their law practice, plantation, or commercial firm had suffered (not to mention their health and disposition) from only a three-month session in the federal city amongst the demagogues, lobbyists, and mosquitoes. Things are rather different these days, when nobody is ever observed leaving Congress less affluent than when he entered. And in the early Republic a former member of the government going on the payroll of a foreign concern or government, if it had even been possible to imagine it, would have been instantly and universally condemned as treason.

The history of national politics up until 1861 is largely the history of a holding action against the "American System," essentially meaning the use of the government to promote private profit by bounties, grants, tariffs, public debt, bank charters, and other instruments of corporate welfare. A less noticed aspect of the struggle against consolidated government that was lost in 1865, though it loomed large in the minds of contemporaries, was the "spoils of office"—the holding of office itself as a source of profit. As in most all matters, the South clung to older practices: being chosen for public trust was a recognition of achievement and of already-existing status. Increasingly in the North, the office itself was sought as the source of status and the pursuit of office bound up in the power of political party machines to buy votes with public money.

More and more as the 19th century wore on, the New Englanders aggressively claimed virtue as their special possession, with the accompanying disdain for others. New England spokesmen, shortly after enacting a 40 per cent tariff protection for their industries, rose in Congress to declare scornfully that the low price of cotton was caused by Southerners' lack of Yankee enterprise. And more and more the sign of virtue became profit-making activity. Whether through genuine private enterprise or rent-seeking (usually some combination of both) did not make much difference.

The belief in superior virtue and virtue as profit-making spread and gathered power over Northern society until it achieved consolidation and institutionalization with Lincoln—the first President elected with no record of achievement or service to the commonwealth, but solely through political management and the promise of payoffs—favorable legislation AND public jobs and contracts. Lincoln's victory not only was a coup for the "American System," establishing a permanent system of welfare for industrialists and bankers. It also brought on a revolutionary expansion of the spoils system.

Whether the Republicans started and kept up the war deliberately for the patronage is debatable, but there is no doubt they embraced their opportunity with the greatest relish. Lincoln's war was a source of profit to large numbers of Northerners quite aside from favorable legislation—a vast array of contractors (some of whom made killings that founded fortunes that still exist today) and beneficiaries of the public payroll. (The Confederate army took new recruits into veteran units from their home territory. The U.S., every time new recruits or conscripts were scraped together, created a new regiment of amateurs. It was not a good idea from the military standpoint, but it was great politics—you could buy a lot of support for the party with new officers' commissions and supply contracts.)

The corruption of the Grant administrations and the Reconstruction state governments was simply a continuance of the same game, without the excuse of shooting war. There followed rapidly a vast pension system for those who had fought to overcome "the rebellion."

For decades Union army pensions was one of the biggest items in the budget. It was the first great American entitlement cornucopia. Little distinction was made between men who had fought the whole war and those who had had on the uniform for six months, or three months, of static service. The paper and wax was all.

In the late 19th and early 20th century, Pecksniff do-gooders promoted "civil service reform," but about all that accomplished was to replace political hacks in government office with unremovable tinpot tyrants determined to use the government to improve the citizens whether the citizens wanted to be improved in that particular way or not. And so it went, until our own day. Americans no longer have a concept of responsibility in public office. The press reports that General Colin Powell is suffering from the "painful blot" on his (inflated) reputation because of his part in bringing on the Iraq debacle. Presumably we are not supposed to condemn lies that are catastrophic for the country, but only to commiserate with the general because his lies have damaged his reputation. Now, as after September 11, 2001, office holders who fail disastrously in their responsibilities to the people are rewarded with promotions, re-election, great increases of money and power, and Presidential medals. It does not even occur to anybody to point out that the pay ought to be for service, not for the paper and wax.

Q & A ON NULLIFICATION
AND INTERPOSITION

Q: What can I read that can give me a serious overview of the true impact of the tariffs of 1828 and 1832 on South Carolina?

A: I think the question of the impact of the protective tariff on South Carolina is the wrong question to ask. It is something of a diversionary tactic, for reasons I will try to explain below.

The questions to ask about that period of American history are

    1) was the protective tariff just?

    2) was it good policy?

    3) was it constitutional?

A believer in free markets and constitutionally limited government can only give a resounding NO to all these questions.

    It was not just South Carolina that objected to the tariff. From the earliest national period John Taylor's writings and John Randolph's speeches, along with many other Southern spokesman, were eloquent and firm on the unjustness of the "protective" tariff. From 1824 on, every Southern legislature strongly condemned the tariff. The only difference was that only South Carolina was willing to go to the extent of actual nullification. This was not because South Carolina had suffered any more than others, but because South Carolina was the only State in which decisions could be made without the input of national party leaders who wanted to avoid hard issues.

    From 1824 on it was apparent that the manufacturers intended a high and permanent system of tariffs, which had not been obvious before, when tariffs had been thought of as revenue measures with perhaps "incidental" protection. The term "lobbyists" was first used in America in the 1820s for the agents of the New England/Pennsylvania manufacturers who began to haunt the legislative halls and hold out inducements to congressmen. The acts of 1828 and 1832 were blatant examples of log-rolling rather than policy decisions. The latter was also deceptively presented by the Jackson/Van Buren forces as a remedy to tariff opponents.

It was not only the South that vigorously opposed the tariffs of 1828 and 1832. The Northern free market men like William Gouge and Condy Raguet exposed the tariff and approved South Carolina's action, and public meetings of Northern merchants and craftsmen denounced the protective tariff as did Democratic conventions in many Northern States at that time and later.

Historians have tried with considerable success to divert the question to an emphasis on South Carolina. The hidden assumption is that the tariff policy is so self-evidently good that there is something peculiar about South Carolina to explain the strong opposition. It must be exhausted soil and declining prosperity (or more recently fears over slavery) that drove South Carolinians to blame their problems on others. This is just a transmission of the claims of the tariffites' propaganda of the time. New Englanders, then as now, were extremely self-centered and self-righteous. They said in Congress that the South's economic problems were because Southerners were, unlike them, lazy and unproductive. (Calhoun pointed out that Southerners produced almost all of the country's foreign trade in an open market while those who complained of Southern lack of enterprise enjoyed a protected domestic market.) Many New England spokesmen said that opposition to such a self-evidently good policy was itself treason. Not nullification, mind you, but opposition to the protective tariff was in itself declared to be treasonous. The historians who concentrate on "the effects on South Carolina" work from a basic assumption that Southerners are too stupid to know their own real interests, are always wrong and deceptive in their politics, and are naturally inclined to be traitors.

So, to approach the question of the tariff as an issue of the peculiarities of South Carolina is a diversion from the larger question of the impact of the tariff on the American economy as a whole. How can any freemarketeer doubt that the impact was unjust? Even more so because it not only benefited one group of people, but it also, on phony grounds of patriotism, diverted wealth from the South to certain interests in the North in a government that was supposed to benefit all parts of the Union. It was this (far more than the slavery issue) that drove Southerners to begin to question the value of the Union. Was the North to get all the benefits and the South to bear all the burdens?

What was the impact of the tariffs on South Carolina? This is an empirical question that, like any complicated situation, can be argued all sorts of ways. It would seem to be axiomatic to advocates of free markets that a government policy that artificially raises the costs of goods for the benefit of a particular interest is harmful. But in a sense that is beside the point. What was the economic effect of the Tea Tax on the American colonists in 1775? The point was that it was an unfair imposition based on an exercise of doubted power.

You can get a good overview of the Southern case from the section on Free Trade in my *The Essential Calhoun*, especially Calhoun's speech on the tariff of 1842. Also my article on "Free Trade..." in the Genovese festschrift, *Slavery, Secession, and Southern History*, edited by Robert Paquette.

Q: How about the constitutional question—is there really no good constitutional argument on behalf of tariffs for protection?

A: There is no question that the Constitution gave certain taxing powers for the purpose of providing the general government with a source of support. The tax on imports was the best way to do this. It was paid by the consumer to the degree of consumption of imported goods, largely luxury items or highly specialized materials and equipment. Equally there is no question that a protective tariff is anti-revenue—using a law for a different purpose than that for which the power had been granted. The Supreme Court held that it was a political question, that it could not look beneath the law itself to its intentions or effects. In the Philadelphia Convention, proposals that the new federal government have the power to lay protective tariffs and to charter corporations failed to carry. As Tom DiLorenzo has recently reminded us, the Hamiltonians cavalierly disregarded the limits on federal power in both these cases in pursuit of their mercantilist, mimic England, agenda. It is perhaps also worth pointing out in this connection that the Constitution absolutely forbade any tax on exports.

Q: And finally, do you believe nullification would have to involve convening a special convention of the people, or could it conceivably be carried out by a state legislature?

A: The South Carolina nullification of 1832 was enacted by a convention of the people especially called for the purpose. By the South Carolina constitution such a convention could only be called by a three/fourths majority of both houses of the legislature. The South Carolinians wanted to make it clear that the act was a high constitutional one—based on the primary sovereignty of the people—like the acts that had made the State independent in 1775 and had ratified the Constitution in 1788. However, the Kentucky and Virginia Resolutions of 1798 and 1799, which laid out the power and right of state interposition against unconstitutional federal acts, were done by the legislatures.

A couple more points. "Nullification" was a derogatory, negative-sounding term invented by the opponents of the right. The proper name is State Interposition.

The historians tell us that Nullification of the tariff by South Carolina failed and federal supremacy was vindicated. That is not quite the truth. One can make a good case that it was a success. The historians note Jackson's proclamation against nullification but they never mention that there was a great outpouring of public opinion against Jackson's proclamation. The proclamation raised the possibility of the coercion of the people of a State by the federal government. Many people, North and South, were more alarmed by that than they were disturbed by nullification. (By the way, Webster DID NOT win the Webster-Hayne Debate. In the Senate, the press, and public opinion, Webster was the clear loser).

Nullification was a success. To defuse the crisis, Congress in 1833 passed the Compromise Tariff by which the tariff would come down by stages over the next ten years after which it would be at a revenue-only. Not bad for a small State against the world. True, the Whigs sought to forget and violate the compromise in 1842 but they did not entirely succeed and the most free-trade tariff in our history was passed in 1846. This would not have happened if it had not been for the action of "our gallant little State."

Q: What is the proper reply to the states which, objecting to the Virginia and Kentucky Resolutions, cited Article III, Section 2 as evidence that the Supreme Court is indeed the arbiter for disputes of power between the federal government and the states?

A: The States that took the position you cite were those deeply invested in Federalist hegemony—devoted to constructing a strong federal judiciary to control what they regarded as the evil and unenlightened masses. They said so very plainly. Was not this position thoroughly repudiated in the Kentucky and Virginia documents themselves, followed immediately by the triumph of the "Principles of 1798" party in the elections? Where does it say that the Supreme Court and not the people have the final say on interpretation?

Calhoun's Carolina

JOHN C. CULHOON. Culhoon is the right pronunciation by the way. John C. Culhoon was an Upcountry man. We upcountry people tend to suspect Charlestonians, like Dr. Tom Fleming, of being somewhat haughty and dissipated. Calhoun studied law briefly in Charleston and found a bride here, and he stopped off when he couldn't avoid it on his way to and from Washington, but he lived in the far western hills as far from Charleston as you could be and still be in South Carolina.

He is buried here, as you may have noted, in the yard of St. Phillips Church. There is a story in that. Having been fortunate in spending nearly every day with this very great man for over 35 years, I have no doubt that he would have preferred to be laid to rest on his own land like Washington, Jefferson, and Jackson.

When his remains were on their way back from Washington City, his family was persuaded to allow him to rest in Charleston temporarily while a suitable monument and final resting place was erected at the Capitol in Columbia. Then the war came and the plans for the monument were never forwarded. In late 1864, when it appeared that Sherman might be headed toward Charleston, the rector and sexton of St. Phillips disinterred the remains and hid them until the war was over. And then there was Reconstruction. There is a place not too far away called the "Calhoun Mansion." It was at one time the residence of one of Calhoun's grandsons but has no connection with the statesman.

There are, of course, many memorials to Calhoun in Charleston, including the Hiram Powers sculpture in City Hall, which was rescued from the bottom of the sea after a shipwreck, and the monument which you may have seen. The monument was erected in the 1880s, during a time of great poverty in the South, by South Carolina ladies who collected small donations from across the South for over 20 years to make it possible. On June 23, 2020, the ignorant mayor and city council of Charleston, using diamond chain saws in a 17-hour operation, took down this Calhoun statue, even though the city does not own the land it was on.

Having had my fun at the expense of the Lowcountry, it is, of course, fitting that we talk about Calhoun's Carolina, our history between the Revolution and the War you have already heard about. Out of diverse origins, the South Carolinians of Calhoun's day created a remarkable unity. In American political history there is nothing like the unity of mind and action that was shown by our gallant little state, as Calhoun called it. During the antebellum era South Carolinians never allowed themselves to be divided by the meaningless contests of national political parties. We were the only state that was able to decide upon and take action on principle without being forced into it by circumstances. We stood alone and unafraid against the powers-that-be in 1832 and won a reduction of the tariff.

In that period, Calhoun was a popular Vice President of the United States. He had been a major American leader since his first speech in the House of Representatives at the age of 29, when he had been recognized, in the words of a leading editor, as "one of those master spirits who leave their stamp on the age in which they live." He did not hesitate to resign the second highest office in the land to represent and defend South Carolina. Demagogues at the time attributed his act, implausibly, to ambition. They said that when Calhoun took snuff, South Carolina sneezed. Such silliness is still retailed by celebrated historians. In reality, the allegiance was mutual. South Carolina supported the great man that it had produced, and he defended the society that had produced him.

Hard as it is to believe today, in the late 1830s the South Carolina legislature refused to accept its share of the so-called "surplus revenue" that was being distributed from the federal treasury to the States on principle—that the money being distributed had been raised by unjust and unconstitutional taxes. That kind of principle no longer exists anywhere in the Union.

But we were, and to some extent still are, at least more than any other state, our own country. We have harbors, rivers, rich soil, forests, factories, hills, plains, great customs and traditions, and fine people—everything we need for a perfectly satisfactory country of our own. Unfortunately, acting in good faith, we made the mistake of joining the Union in 1788, and we have been exploited by stronger outside powers ever since. In our last effort to get out from under them, we mobilized 90 per cent of our male citizens and lost a fourth of them.

Antebellum Charleston had a rich intellectual and artistic culture, much more worthy than Boston/New York centered official opinion has allowed. And South Carolina, in its unity, had genuine diversity. The Catholic Bishop of Charleston, John England, was a leading American prelate and was invited to address the legislature at a time when convents were being destroyed by mobs in Boston and Philadelphia.

When I think of the solidarity of free allegiance within diversity that marked Calhoun's South Carolina, I think of the clergy of Charleston who met and mingled on free and friendly terms and were at one where the interest of their state was concerned. Bishop England, the Baptist leader Furman, the Methodist bishop Capers, several noted Presbyterian clergymen, the Lutheran pastor John Bachman who was also a world-famous naturalist, noted Episcopalians including the theologian James Warley Miles whose works were read in Europe and who was the master of thirty languages, Rabbi Myers. And perhaps most telling: The Rev. Samuel and Mrs. Caroline Gilman, Unitarians from Massachusetts. His career in Charleston was a steady progress toward orthodoxy, and Caroline, a talented writer, published a defense of the South in reply to *Uncle Tom's Cabin*.

In the years before the war, any of them could have been seen in Russell's Bookstore—along with William Gilmore Simms, the poets Henry Timrod and Paul Hamilton Hayne, the first historian of American diplomacy William Henry Trescot, and any of a number of artists and scientific gentlemen who were widely known at the time.

I could talk about Calhoun for the rest of the year, but I am allowed only a few minutes. I could talk about his "Disquisition on Government," which is as profound an examination of human nature, society, government, and constitutions as ever written by an American and which rests, in part, on the experience of South Carolina in achieving consensus in freedom. I could talk about his understanding of Constitution and Union and efforts to preserve them in their original nature.

But I will instead point to Calhoun's profound and prophetic statesmanship in less familiar matters—a prime exhibit of republican virtue on which this country was founded, and which has long ago disappeared. Calhoun saw it disappearing long before Lincoln killed it for good. What Calhoun's words tell us about many aspects of political economy, about questions of war and peace, about the nature and destiny of the American experiment, might persuade that he is the ideal republican statesman produced and upheld by the ideal republic that was South Carolina. And what he has to say is as relevant at this moment as it was when he spoke.

Remarks at the John Randolph Club Annual Meeting, December 9 & 10, 2005 in Charleston, South Carolina.

MARGARET COIT'S
JOHN C. CALHOUN, AMERICAN PORTRAIT

DURING THE GREAT MIDDLE PERIOD of American history between Jefferson's presidency and the Civil War, the legacy of the Founding Fathers clashed and mingled with the historical force of modernization and a geometric explosion of population, territory, economy, and culture. Out of this formative period—complex, varied, and problematic—emerged a synthesis that is the America we have known until recently The period coincides with the career of John C. Calhoun as a national statesman.

From 1811 to 1850—as representative from South Carolina, secretary of war, vice president, twice presidential contender, secretary of state, and senator for fifteen years—Calhoun was a central figure in the American experience. He was never predominant in influence, even in the South in his own lifetime, but there was never a time when he was not a major player who had to be taken into account.

He had many admirers and disciples, northern as well as southern, but he never enjoyed a large political base, an effective party organization, significant power over patronage, or national mass popularity. For most of his career he was either outside the two-party system or at odds with the leadership of the party with which he was identified. Despite the absence of all these hallmarks of political power, from the beginning to the end of his forty-year career Calhoun arrested public attention and influenced public opinion. Calhoun had a major if not always decisive influence on every issue of the period—in regard not only to state-federal conflict and slavery, with which he is most commonly associated by later generations, but also to free trade and tariff, banking and currency, taxation and expenditure, war and peace, foreign relations, Indian policy, the public lands, internal improvements, the two-party system, and the struggle between congressional and presidential power.

With Henry Clay and Daniel Webster, Calhoun made up "The Great Triumvirate," which, as Merrill D. Peterson has reminded us in a recent work of that name, for forty years; "triangulated the destiny of the nation." Together with General Andrew Jackson (whom the triangle was largely designed to contain), the Great Triumvirate were American political life between that time when Jefferson crossed the Potomac going South for the last time, leaving behind a modest federal establishment for a Union of the States, and that time when Lincoln, with the help of Generals Grant and Sherman, forged the modern American state out of blood and fire.

Calhoun was, then, as every one at the time and later recognized, a major protagonist in the drama of expansion and conflict that is at the heart and center of American history in the nineteenth century. Whatever road one travels, Vernon L. Parrington observed in *Main Currents in American Thought*, one finds Calhoun standing at the crossroads. And while Calhoun is very far from being the most admired of American statesmen, and in some calculations is one of the great villains of American history, it is curiously true that never at any time, during his life or since, has he lacked weighty admirers, who often appear from quite unexpected quarters.

But Calhoun has an additional importance not shared with the other great public men of his time or later and in which he resembles the generation of the Founding Fathers. Though a public man speaking on pressing public issues, Calhoun always cast his political positions and arguments in principled and philosophical terms and always disdained the superficial and opportunistic view for the long-range one. As Margaret Coit observes in her summation of Calhoun's career (p. 516): "He had been a statesman, not a politician."

Calhoun was, then, a political thinker as well as a political actor, and this has given him a certain enduring and even prophetic quality. Calhoun qua political thinker has received continuing, international, and interdisciplinary interest from diverse generations, countries, and viewpoints. Except for Jefferson and Lincoln, it is hard to think of any

American statesman who has had admirers from more points of the compass and the political spectrum, and for reasons that transcend the issues of his own time, than has Calhoun.

Margaret Coit knows this, and it is significant that her account of Calhoun's life and ideas has been admired by both Arthur M. Schlesinger, Jr., the paragon of American liberal historians, and Russell Kirk, the dean of modern American conservative thinkers. In their company is President John F. Kennedy, who included *John C. Calhoun: American Portrait* on the list of his ten favorite political biographies.

Calhoun's importance has always been evident but has not always been readily acknowledged in some quarters. That we can now assert with confidence and without fear of successful contradiction Calhoun's enduring importance as a political thinker is in part due to the achievement represented by *John C. Calhoun: American Portrait*.

The timing of the revival of interest in and appreciation for Calhoun at the midpoint of the twentieth century was significant. In the years after world War II many Americans were in a mood to be receptive to old wisdom that might shed some light on pressing and troubling problems of democracy—problems of consensus, pluralism, economic concentration, and minority rights.

"Miss Coit's book provides far and away the most detailed, vivid, and convincing personal characterization of Calhoun we have," wrote Schlesinger in 1950 on the first appearance of *John C. Calhoun: American Portrait*.[1] The passage of four decades and a Niagara of additional published material on the great Southern statesman leaves no reason to reverse Schlesinger's judgment, a judgment confirmed by the award of the 1951 Pulitzer Prize for Biography.

Another early reviewer, Gerald W. Johnson, agreed: "The book has many merits—learning, logical form, obvious sincerity, lucidity... The net result is that she has taken what is commonly regarded as one of the driest stories in American history and turned it into a colorful, somberly gorgeous portrait that enthralls the attention and stirs the

---

1 *Nation* (April 1, 1950), 170:302.

emotions as few modern biographies do."[2] High praise for the first book of a young newspaperwoman, barely out of her twenties and with no advanced degrees in history, but entirely justified. That the book contains the best extant characterization of Calhoun does not exhaust its merits. It presents a vivid history of Calhoun's times. To quote another early reviewer: "Miss Coit has the art of creating historical characters of almost Shakespearean stature: not only Calhoun of the tortured doubts, intense affections, discouragements, but also the men who ruled with him, Jackson, Webster, Clay."[3] The book also contains an original and arresting interpretation of Calhoun's ideas and their continuing relevance for later times.

Further, it is a wonderful example of historical work of an increasingly rare type—a work that speaks equally to the general and the scholarly reader. Claude G. Bowers, probably the most successful American popular historian of the first half of the twentieth century, hailed the biography on its publication as "a brilliant achievement, scholarly and at the same time a work of art steeped in charm."[4] The reading and re-reading of *John C. Calhoun: American Portrait* can actually be enjoyed by a large and varied audience, which is sadly untrue of the productions of most academic historians, in 1950 or later.

Coit's deep and sympathetic recovery of the most Southern of all statesmen is all the more surprising when we remember that she is a New England native, though raised and educated in North Carolina. The combination of contrasting influences proved a happy one. While pursuing a career in big-city journalism after graduation from the Woman's College of the University of North Carolina (now the University of North Carolina at Greensboro) on the eve of World War II, Coit undertook the audacious assignment of a thorough biography of one of the most difficult and contentious figures in American history. Even more audaciously, the biography was not to be a quick publisher's knockdown. It was to be based on extensive scholarly

---

2 *New York Herald Tribune Book Review*, March 5, 1950, p. 1.
3 Clorinda Clarke in *Catholic World* (July 1950), 171:316.
4 *New York Times Book Review*, March 5, 1950, p. 1.

research, incorporate both narrative and interpretation, appeal to both general readers and scholars, and have contemporary relevance as well as historical interest.

The result was a classic of the biographer's craft which remains the best one-volume treatment of its subject. *John C. Calhoun: American Portrait* has been a remarkable success that has gone through many printings in hardback and paperback.

Coit has since published a number of other books on the "Jacksonian" era of American history, as well as a prize-winning biography of another difficult subject, Bernard Baruch, in 1958. Leaving journalism, she was for some years professor at Fairleigh Dickinson University in New Jersey. She now lives with her husband, Albert Elwell, farmer and poet, at Strawberry Hill in West Newbury, Massachusetts, where she is active in local affairs and has been moderator of the town meeting. All of Coit's books are marked by independence of thought, original historical insight, and good writing.

Even though conditions were in some respects favorable, the task of redeeming Calhoun's personality from distortion and his political thought from neglect and condescension in the middle of the twentieth century was formidable. As Coit wrote (p. 382): "With the possible exception of George Washington, no American statesman has been more thoroughly dehumanized than John C. Calhoun."

The Calhoun fixed almost indelibly in American folklore and even in widespread "scholarly" understanding was still the dour and fanatical "cast-iron man" of the English writer Harriet Martineau, who knew him only slightly. This Calhoun stared out of the textbooks (as indeed he often still does) from the Matthew Brady daguerreotype taken near the end of his life when he was wasted by disease, to frighten generations of northern schoolchildren: the evil genius who personified the perfidy of the South, and so obviously looked the part.

It was always a superficial image, designed to bolster the confidence of the winning side in the Civil War. But it was Margaret Coit who more than any other writer gave it the "coup de grace" and restored to the national consciousness the real Calhoun—the handsome, brilliant, patriotic, charming figure who was known to most of his contemporaries for most of his life.

For there was a Calhoun, as Coit shows us, whose influence depended upon personal charm and impregnable integrity, next only to intellect, and who at any time could win the undying admiration of army officers or intellectuals or hard-fisted labor leaders, or even, sometimes, unwilling young abolitionists.

There was a Calhoun who was most happy when engaged in the pursuits of a farmer; who was the too-indulgent father of many children; who had such a characteristically American enthusiasm for technology and material progress that in his fifties he spent nine days on horseback clambering over the most rugged part of the Appalachians to satisfy himself as to the best route for a railroad; who could charmingly whisper verses in the ear of President Tyler's young bride, to set her at ease during her first state dinner. Most of all, there was the tragic patriot who struggled heroically, not to destroy the Union but to find a way to save it from the chaos of clashing imperatives.

Coit restored to our national pantheon this lost figure, surely a constructive and consoling achievement. Her book was probably the decisive factor in the United States Senate's designating Calhoun as one of its five greats in 1959, on the finding of a committee chaired by John F. Kennedy.

If one wished to criticize *John C. Calhoun: American Portrait*, one might suggest that this redemption was achieved at the price of a certain amount of romanticism and imaginative amplification of bare fact. This was a line taken by a few reviewers at the time of the book's first publication, though the critical reception, in both academic and popular journals, was overwhelmingly positive.[5]

Where adequate documentary evidence is and forever will be lacking—for instance, in regard to Calhoun's childhood, his relationship with his wife, and his encounters with Thomas Jefferson—Coit has

---

5 *Book Review Digest,* 1950, pp. 188-189.

supplied us with a plausible version of what can never be known for sure. We are always aware that this is what she is doing. The pedantic critics took too narrow a view of what history is and how it should be written. It is not a question of accurate or inaccurate, it is a question of the proper strategy for presentation of an inescapably imperfect documentary record.

We do not know, for instance, from direct evidence, what suit Calhoun wore on a particular occasion of a great and dramatic speech in the Senate. But we do know, from direct evidence, what sort of suit he is likely to have worn, and are entitled to say so without too much quibbling. Contrary to what many pedants seem to think, literal mindedness is not at all the same thing as truth. What is important is the historian's integrity and responsibility in determining probabilities where there are no certainties.

History must adhere to the documentary record. This is what distinguishes it from other forms of examination of the human experience. But no great history, certainly no successful narrative history, has ever been written without the use of the imagination. Facts do not tell their own story. They have meaning only in a relationship to a total picture which is, in part, a product of the historian's imaginative arrangement. To put it another way, the line between fact and imagination is real and significant but not absolute, any more than is, as we know from modern physics, the line between time and motion.

It is the loss of this basic truth of historical knowledge, a truth that has always informed the greatest historians, that renders so much historical output, unlike *John C. Calhoun: American Portrait*, unreadable to the non-specialist and bereft of cultural significance, human impact, and enduring meaning.

I have defended this book from a charge of romanticism because the charge has been made from time to time, but the defense is not really necessary. We would have to look far and wide to find a more controlled and responsible and creative exercise of the historical imagination. As another early reviewer commented, Coit makes "it possible for any reasonable reader to reach a reasonable conclusion.[6] Having spent two decades in intimate daily communion with the hard documentary record of Calhoun, I find only few and minor errors (such as can be found in any ambitious work) and few and minor places to take issue with in Coit's account of Calhoun's life and personality. Any significant points of disagreement I have with the book have to do with the larger historical context, the inevitable disagreements a thoughtful historian will have with any work on a period with which he or she is familiar.

And even where I am not in accord I am compelled to recognize *John C. Calhoun: American Portrait* as a significant, original, and persuasive interpretation of the period of American history that is the least amenable to simple synthesis and that is littered with the debris of historiographical dispute.

Many historians of recent day prefer the quantitative and literal and eschew the kind of deep cultural background that suffuses this biography. For them Coit is out of step. For instance, she describes Southern society as a fusion of the low country aristocrat and the Celtic backcountryman, an image that she uses to account for both Calhoun and Andrew Jackson. Before we dismiss this as poetic license, we should note that she has merely anticipated by four decades an extremely sophisticated recent cultural history of American origins, which elaborately, with a vast array of evidence, makes the same point. (I refer to David Hackett Fischer's *Albion's Seed: Four British Folkways in America*.)

One suspects that what some critics mean by romanticism is simply that Coit finds Calhoun a sympathetic figure and is willing to give him the benefit of a reasonable doubt. They find this ideologically unacceptable, because the great evil genius of the South must not be treated sympathetically. But an equally romanticized negative treatment would be quite acceptable; and this is, indeed, what has

---

6   A. B. Miller in *Annals of the American Academy* (November 1950), 272:219.

often happened in Calhoun biography and in the treatment of Calhoun in works on the "Jacksonian" era, both before and after the publication of *John C. Calhoun: American Portrait.*

Calhoun's most recent biographer, for example, makes the completely subjective judgment that Calhoun was "out of touch with reality" at the time of the Nullification crisis.[7] This estimate reflects the propaganda of some of his opponents at the time. But Calhoun was not out of touch with reality; he simply viewed reality in a different framework than did ordinary pragmatic politicians. In the Nullification crisis, though he did not completely carry the day, Calhoun fought all the powers arrayed against him—all three branches of the federal government, both major political parties, overwhelming public opinion, and the formidable temper and popularity of Andrew Jackson—down to a compromise of the issue that most concerned him. No small accomplishment for a political leader "out of touch with reality."

Coit's biography is subjective in that she is sympathetically engaged with her subject. But her historianship compares favorably with many works on the "Jacksonian" period which are accepted by academic historians without cavil, apparently because their subjectivism is in the service not of Calhoun but of a romanticized "Jacksonian democracy." The book provides a ready and persuasive antidote for such accounts.

The work should surely redeem Calhoun, for all time, from the sillier charges of ambition and opportunism that have marked much of the literature about him. One conventional school of interpretation portrays Calhoun's career as explained by an overwhelming lust for the presidency—to the degree that Gerald M. Capers entitled his 1960 biography *John C. Calhoun: Opportunist.*

Coit provides a more complex and plausible account. Opportunism is a strange description for a public man, widely admired, who resigned the vice presidency, to which he had been twice elected by large

---

7   John Niven, *John C. Calhoun and the Price of Union: A Biography* (Baton Rouge: Louisiana State University Press, 1988). A comprehensive evaluation of the writing on Calhoun can be found in Clyde N. Wilson, *John C. Calhoun: A Bibliography* (Westport, Conn. & London: Meckler, 1990).

majorities, to accompany his own small state in a dangerous pursuit of principle. It should be clear that something other than conventional ambition governed the actions of such a man. Coit comes the closest of any of Calhoun's many biographers to giving us an understanding of what that was. In so doing, she helps to redeem a whole era of American history from distortion.

A little less difficult but perhaps more important than Coit's recovery of Calhoun the man was her recovery of Calhoun the political thinker. The outcome of the Civil War had fixed an image of Calhoun as a fanatic whose intellect was bent to the one indefensible goal of preserving slavery. The first serious biography after the Civil War, that of the German-American Hermann E. von Holst (*John C. Calhoun*, 1881), pursued this theme relentlessly, even though there was in his book itself evidence against so oversimplified a view of American history.

Yet, as preposterous as it now seems, such a view, though not unchallenged, long held sway. Holst dealt with the polemics of the sectional struggle of the late antebellum period. He knew nothing of the ancient and important role that state rights had played in the American mind, nor of the early history of slavery. With much superior historical scope, Coit reminds us that the young Calhoun was educated in a Connecticut where slavery was still known and state rights still preached by many.

In the recovery of the complexities and timeless elements of Calhoun's ideas, *John C. Calhoun: American Portrait* had substantial allies. As early as 1927, in a work called *The American Heresy*, the English writer Christopher Hollis had linked Calhoun with Jefferson, Lincoln, and Wilson as the great definers of the American regime.

There was also Charles M. Wiltse's careful and detailed study of the life in political context (*John C. Calhoun*, 3 vols., 1944-1951). Wiltse's portrayal of the modern relevance of Calhoun's thought was his own, but in most respects was compatible with Coit's.

August O. Spain's *The Political Theory of John C. Calhoun*, a dispassionate exposition, appeared the year after *John C. Calhoun: American Portrait*. At about the same time Coit began her work,

Robert L. Meriwether started collecting and planning at the University of South Carolina for a comprehensive edition of *The Papers of John C. Calhoun.*

At about the same time, there was a host of writers, popular and scholarly, on both sides of the Atlantic, who began in articles to point to Calhoun as a prophet of enduring significance and with concrete application to the plight of men and nations in an era of class conflict, economic concentration, totalitarianism, and global strife. The stature that Calhoun had achieved was indicated by the title of a celebrated 1948 article in political science: "A Key to American Politics: Calhoun's Pluralism,"[8] and by Felix Morley's 1951 book, *Freedom and Federalism,* which strenuously argued Calhoun's relevance to the situation of America in the twentieth century.

By mid-century, serious thinkers, whether they admired Calhoun or not, no longer viewed him as only the defender of a peculiar outmoded and beleaguered sectional interest. Not every one would have taken the claim for Calhoun as far as did Coit, but they would have understood the point: "Calhoun stands in the first rank of men America has produced. For as thinker and prophet, he was more important for later times than for his own" (p. 531).

Most earlier biographers had restricted their treatment of Calhoun's political thought largely to questions of constitutional interpretation in regard to slavery and state rights. Coit was quite right, and in good company, in avoiding this trap and portraying Calhoun as a statesman of broad views and interests. Calhoun made more speeches on banking and currency, and on protection and free trade, than he did on slavery, and for most of his career economic issues loomed larger than sectional conflict.

A number of economic historians have, in fact, found Calhoun's grasp of fiscal and monetary policy superior to that of other public figures of his day. Neither Coit nor any other writer has yet completely exhausted all that might be said about Calhoun's political economy. This remains a fruitful line of research for the alert. But Coit struggles

---

8 Peter F. Drucker in *Review of Politics* (October 1948), 10:412-426.

mightily to bring the complex knot of issues involving banking, currency, the tariff, and other aspects of economic conflict and development, under our understanding. This is in stark contrast with many other biographers, who do not seem to be aware that Calhoun had a fully developed political economy, distinct from that of both the Democrats and the Whigs, and who tend to treat such issues merely as political tactics.

Historical understanding, unfortunately, is not always cumulative. We do not necessarily always progress to more sophisticated and inclusive interpretations, and we sometimes discover that old works are not, after all, superseded. We need to go back now and then and recover insights that have been lost. That we can do splendidly in this work.

One, though not the only, virtue of Coit's treatment of Calhoun as a political thinker, a treatment skillfully developed against the narrative of his life, is precisely the fact that the book is very much a product of its time, the immediate post-World War II era. As such, it instructs us usefully not only about Calhoun but also about certain lost alternatives that flourished in the intellectual climate of a few decades ago.

Coit's Calhoun, slavery aside, is an adherent neither of the welfare state nor of big business. He is, rather, the advocate of another way, of what used to be known as Jeffersonian Democracy. Coit's Calhoun is a conservative Democrat who, if we may be permitted an anachronistic reference, would not have been satisfied with either a Reagan or a Mondale, and who would not have agreed that between them they subsumed all the policy alternatives available to America. So far as participation in the national dialogue goes, the breed of Jeffersonian Democrat appears almost extinct. However, a specimen can still be sighted now and then in the hinterland, and there may be a great many more of them out there than is currently believed. At any rate, for historical perspective we badly need to be reminded that they loom very large indeed in the American record; were once, in fact, the predominant national type. Coming at the time and from the direction that it did, this book provides us with insight into certain forgotten potentialities of its own time as well as Calhoun's and reminds us of a tradition that links both and that is perhaps even yet not quite dead.

Here it may be useful to remember Calhoun's own long-range view of political victories, as summarized by Coit: "The potential success of a cause had nothing whatever to do with its abstract merits." John C. Calhoun is an important and problematic figure at the heart of American history and a prophet of whose ideas we can usefully take account in our present concerns. This book is the best place to begin a study of the subject. That is true despite many turns of the wheel of history since it was written and will likely remain true whatever turns of the wheel of history are to come.

[Margaret Coit Elwell passed away in 2003 at the age of 83.]

Introduction to a new edition of John C. Calhoun: American Portrait. *University of South Carolina Press, 2007.*

The Concurrent Majority

IN ANY DISCUSSION OF FEDERALISM—at least among that minority whose substantive knowledge of American principles and ideals precedes the beginning of the Kennedy dynasty—the name of John C. Calhoun and his idea of the concurrent majority is likely to come up.

Calhoun's reputation as a political thinker has had its ups and downs. Widely praised in his own time and after, by no means solely by defenders of slavery and state rights, he was dismissed as a narrow reactionary fanatic during the intellectual rationalization of the victory in the Civil War. That victory, among other things, implied the triumph of the programmatically implemented will of the majority, in which ideas of Constitutional limitations and minority rights had only token place. In the 1950's, however, in biographies and commentaries from surprisingly diverse quarters, Calhoun was rediscovered and elevated. The burden of this rediscovery is conveyed by the title of one of many scholarly articles of the time, Peter Drucker's "Calhoun's Pluralism: A Key to American Politics." Calhoun was celebrated as the philosopher and prophet of minority rights. His idea of the concurrent majority, implying the necessity to secure the assent of significant minorities for major political decisions, was thought of as having described the way American pluralism actually worked.

During the Civil Rights Revolution, Calhoun was relegated to a minor and negative role. Recently, as a part of the broad movement of conservatism, he has once more been receiving favorable attention. He has been so treated in Italian and Japanese scholarly journals. In American books and journals he has been called upon to provide solutions for the problems of the United Nations, Northern Ireland, and South Africa, and his ideas have been invoked to support Supreme Court decisions favoring minority representation on local governing bodies and even as a potential resource for Black Americans.

There is some merit and usefulness in these formulations. However, they slight and distort the real burden of Calhoun's thinking on American government. For these formulations only incompletely grasp what Calhoun had to say, and, in my opinion, they sometimes embody a Pollyannish and inaccurate notion of the way our government works. These formulations, which Calhoun's realism would have scorned, in fact represent the tendency of current thinkers to transcribe into mechanical and ideological terms ideas that are basically moral. Calhoun is better viewed as the last of the great republican thinkers who reached their peak with the Founding Fathers rather than as a prophet of modem pluralism, as a philosopher of democratic consent rather than as an architect of minority rights.

Calhoun's thought, embodied in 40 years of congressional speeches and public papers and in his two treatises, *A Disquisition on Government* and *A Discourse on the Constitution and Government of the United States*, constitutes a remarkable body of commentary on the American system—its political economy, finance, international affairs, and many other matters, as well as Constitutional principles. Calhoun was the last active American statesman who was philosophical rather than empirical. To fully elucidate this would take several books. Here I wish to do no more than point to the opening pages of *A Disquisition on Government and A Discourse on the Constitution and Government of the United States*. Properly understood, they contain a wealth of insight pertinent to the recovery of Old Federalism.

A Disquisition on Government, a slim 100 pages, is the most considered of Calhoun's works, to which he devoted his leisure in the last five years of his life. He said that he hoped by it "to lay a solid foundation for political science." Simple and clear in style, the work is complex enough in implications to have provoked many different interpretations. It would be an accurate, though not a complete, description to say that it is a study of the nature of the consent of the governed in a government of people.

A reading of the *Disquisition* afresh should convince anyone that Calhoun's concurrent majority was not, in the first instance, structural. It was not, except incidentally, a series of devices to protect minority rights, though such devices, given a Constitutional system that already relied on checks and balances, had some relevance. What Calhoun was interested in was the nature of consent. All agreed that American government rested upon the consent of the governed, that this was the starting point for a democratic society. But what was this consent? How was it to be expressed, measured, and preserved? This, to Calhoun, related less to cheeks and balances and the mechanical features of government than to the old republican question of the virtue of the people. It is here that Calhoun has his real relevance. He was attempting to purify and clarify the republican idea of the consent of the governed, to move it to higher ground where it would be safe from the pressures of the 19th century that were silently turning it upside down. In this he failed, but nonetheless is still instructive.

In the *Disquisition*, Calhoun not only argues for his own views, but also recapitulates the implicit assumptions of the Founders of the American Constitution-making period.

Man is inescapably born a social animal. Without society he can scarcely exist much less realise his potential. But individual man also has selfish instincts which can trouble his fellows in society. Thus something, usually called "government," is needed to keep the peace and enforce justice. But those who hold the power to do these good things are also individual selfish men and need to be restrained. The restraints on power can take many forms but are essentially expressed in a "constitution" which defines and enforces the limits of power.

We like to think of our democracy as having sprung naturally from the political wisdom of the philosophical revolutionists and Constitution-makers of our founding period. We, like they, believe that government rests properly on the consent of the governed, the will of the people. However, when we contemplate modern ideas of the relationship between the democratic state and the people with the degree of historical perspective provided by Calhoun's *Disquisition*, we confront at once an innovative assumption that has crept into our thinking and turned the understanding of the Fathers on its head.

As expounded in the 20th century, the theory of democracy is that the rule of the people is the sum of individual wills and inclinations. The democratic man casts his vote, along with all the other citizens, and the numerical majority of these votes determine the will of the people. By this scheme the chief focus of social value is the democratic process itself—the right of participation and the possibility of the minority becoming a majority at the next election. This description seems to me to fairly represent the theory of American politics as it has been described in the last half-century or so by the predominant academic political scientists and popular spokesmen.

Under this dispensation, a great deal that was assumed as basic in the republican philosophy of the Founding Fathers gets lost. What is to be decided by the will of the people, directly or by representatives, for instance, is usually seen as programmatic and empirical. The public good has no independent existence but is the sum of trade-offs between the union member, the manufacturer, the public school teacher, the welfare client, and all the other participants in the process. The will of the people thus becomes a balance of interests, a sharing of the pie. Not only is the idea of the public good, taken for granted by the Founders and by Calhoun, missing here, but also missing is the idea of the independent citizen whose strenuous virtue is the foundation of the public good.

By this scheme, the citizen is defined and exists by virtue of his participation in the democratic collectivity. In fact, only in its emphasis on "openness" does this idea of the democratic society differ from modern totalitarian theory. In both, the state and the individual confront each other starkly, and the individual, in the final analysis, is defined by the state. But for the Founding Fathers, the bedrock of republicanism was not the egalitarian political participation of the abstract individual so dear to modern democratic theory. Rather, republicanism (government of the people) was defined by the freedom and self-determination of communities of men, preexisting historically in all the complexity and differentiation of their social bonds. The history of American democracy is, until the 20th century, the history of community. Self-government was the expression, not of the individual, but of communities. Missing from the modern formulation is the assumption with which Calhoun began—preexistent society itself.

For the Founders, liberty was not the right of the rootless individual to do as he pleased or to participate in a process of inevitably corrupt head-counting leading to majority rule. It was, rather, the right of natural communities to be free from the depredations of the state. The definition of tyranny in the republican philosophy (inherited from the English "country party" amplified by Colonial American experience and thought, and underlying the American Revolution) was the overreaching by the state of its legitimate bounds to tamper with or exploit the communities of men. The point of Constitution was not that they guaranteed a process of democratic decision-making. It was, rather, that society (the people) created and delimited an authority for its protection. In theory and practice, we have moved from a condition in which majority rule was a device for protecting society from the state, to one in which society is the raw material to be exploited and reconstructed by the state, acting in the name of a "majority."

It was this which Calhoun foresaw when he spoke with contempt of the "mere numerical majority." Here, I submit, is an insight of great importance. For Calhoun was not simply advocating a veto power for a numerical minority within a political system governed by a numerical majority. His point was much more basic. It was that the "numerical majority" or the "mere majority" did not represent the consent of the governed, that the political will of the people properly involved not head-counting but something higher and more intangible, a process of *consent* by society. But here is the key point. The elements of this consent were the organic parts of society, preexistent to government. These elements, being the product of society, and not of the state, ought to be inviolate. It was these elements that deserved the protection of the veto power implicit in the concurrent majority. Throughout Calhoun's discussion is the recognition of the superiority of the natural social elements, those that have come into existence spontaneously by the force of history and the necessities of man's nature, over those artificially created or enhanced by government action. The latter are precisely seen as one of the dangerous by-products of an unqualified and abstract majority.

In any proper theory of democratic government, society must precede the state. It is with this observation that Calhoun begins. Society was man as he was found—in family, in custom, in ethnic, territorial, religious, and occupational communities. For Calhoun, and here he was simply restating the assumptions of the Founders, the locus of value was not in the democratic process, it was in society. The democratic process was merely the best means to protect and preserve society. That society is hierarchical and antiegalitarian in both structure and values does not contradict the fact that communities should largely govern themselves and give the law to the state. And there is no protection implied for minorities which seek to come into being or power by state action. No ground is laid here for a pluralism marked by claims to veto power on the part of minorities who wish to disrupt natural society or assert an inviolate right to the earnings of others by state action (e.g., the advocates of "gay rights" and of "welfare rights").

It was Calhoun's assumption, rather, that such artificial minorities threatened the consensual basis of the government of the people. He decried particularly in his own time manufacturers (by virtue of log-rolling a numerical majority) who wished to force industry into prosperity through protective tariffs that preyed upon the earnings of other parts of the community and political spoilsmen who sought the profits and power of office rather than the public good. In the latter connection he spoke again and again on the corruption of democratic consent represented by empty party slogans (like the Whigs' "Tippecanoe and Tyler, too" of 1840) and by the rise of oily equivocators like Martin Van Buren, who sought to mute and obscure issues, to rest their appeal on the broadest and least controversial ground possible, and thus to achieve power as an end in itself rather than as a means to reach fundamental decisions for the public good.

One might argue, as Daniel Boorstin has, that this muting of issues was a pragmatic and constructive avoidance of dangerous antagonisms. This is a kind of evasive pragmatism that would have been anathema to both Jefferson and Hamilton. The effect of this blandness, Calhoun maintained, was to undermine that free deliberation *within and among* communities that was a necessity for achieving the genuine consent of the people. The end result was to suppress disagreements that might be honourably adjusted, force them into other channels, and postpone and increase the explosion. Thus Calhoun predicted that the evasions of party men would lead to civil war, and those historians who have characterized the Civil War as a failure of democracy must concur.

Put another way, the consent of the governed was not to be viewed primarily as a process of counting heads, even when conditioned by technical safeguards for the minority. The consent of the governed was primarily a high moral matter—a process of political deliberation and social assent. The minority veto was not a device to block decision, but an effort to provoke further deliberation and a higher consensus. It trusted in the consent of the governed, that is, in the people, to find the right answers, provided the action of a mere majority, which might be a temporary manifestation of selfish combinations, could be suspended long enough to bring into play the higher consensus of communities.

Reflect upon the degree to which democracy depends upon the spirit of parliamentary institutions—the agreement that opponents are to be heard, to be dealt with civilly, and not to be overridden ruthlessly; that all are bound by decisions made after a proper hearing; and that all are pledged to remain a community even in disagreement. This entire proceeding relates less to the theory of majority rule, head-counting, than it does to the moral heritage of feudal chivalry—tolerance and respect for the opponent as bound within a common system of honour. There is nothing about it that is modern, utilitarian, or efficient. If the consensus is to be maintained, there are things the mere numerical majority must not do, even when it has the power. The majority must look for an answer that is inclusive and morally satisfactory rather than expedient, the morally satisfactory answer being, in the long run, also the most practical if genuine consent of the governed is to be maintained.

Here, then, is the lesson. The community must be the master of the state rather than its raw material. This is indeed a logical necessity in any viable theory of self-government, as well as a Constitutional and moral truth. It is also, I believe, an historical truth. Calhoun's postulate that society precedes government is not, like the state of nature, merely a convenient theoretical starting point. It actually describes the origins of American government and provides the element that distinguishes America from Old World societies. In a speech of 1841, Calhoun referred to a historical contingency which "through the mysterious dispensation of Providence" had had a decisive effect on "the prosperity and greatness of our country." This contingency was that British America was not settled by an armed government, but "by hardy and enterprising emigrants, inspired, in some instances, with a holy zeal to preserve their religious faith in its purity; in others, by the love of adventure and gain; and in all, with a devotion to liberty. It is to settlements formed by individuals so influenced, and thrown, from the beginning, on their own resources almost exclusively, that we owe our enterprise, energy, love of liberty, and capacity for self-government."

When Calhoun premised that society preceded government, he was merely recalling American experience. His own family was part of a kith of Scotch-Irishmen who had come into the upcountry of South Carolina before the Revolution when it was empty of all but hostile Indians, tied together not by the state but by blood, religion, necessity, and the desire to make a new life. They carried some cultural baggage, and there was a distant Crown that was in theory sovereign. But the settlers were in fact virtually self-governing and self-reliant communities in economic, political, ecclesiastical, and military affairs. There was a real sense in which they participated in the creation of their own governments and constitutions by communal acts of consent.

The South Carolina county in which I now live was occupied at the beginning of the American Revolution by interconnected families of prosperous German farmers. They had been settled for half a century and had no particular quarrel with the King in Great Britain. When confronted with the Revolution they did not appeal to the rights of individual man. The heads of households gathered under the trees, talked for two days, and decided that the interest of their community would best be served by allegiance to the independence cause, which they thereafter supported loyally, often at the cost of property and life. If this seems an exaggerated or eccentric statement of historical precedence of society over government in this continent, reflect upon the self-governing congregations of Puritans who settled Massachusetts Bay, on the self-governing wagon trains and mining camps of the West, and on the later communities of immigrants of many sorts. Nowhere does the individual constitute only an abstract integer in a numerical majority.

There is a sense, of course, in which the subjugation of society to government, the reversal of the master-servant relationship between the community and the state apparatus, was an ineluctable product of "modernization:' But there is also a sense in which it was a conscious decision, and therefore reversible. For, at an identifiable point in our history, we *decided* that the state ought to become master. This happened at the end of the 19th century, when a Progressive elite declared that the conditions of modernity required it to take a guardian role through the Federal government and discard previous notions of what constituted American principles. I can illustrate this turning point by a typical assertion of that time that I happen to have conveniently at hand. It is from the founding statement of the American Economic Association in 1885: "We regard the state as an agency whose positive assistance is one of the indispensable conditions of human progress." That is, the community is no longer able to govern itself, but must be guided by a class of experts wielding the power of the state. But the complexity of modern society did not necessarily call for a shift to the state. It called for new instruments of consensus formation. Empowering the state to solve all our problems does not make the state the instrument of the people. It makes the state, and this was Calhoun's point about the "numerical majority," the instrument of the strongest interests and reduces democracy to an endless game of pie-sharing and the citizen to an abstraction.

The United States already had an indirectly elected Senate; bills that must be read thrice before passage; an indirectly elected President with a veto power; and an independent judiciary. And all this merely to alleviate majority rule in a government that was itself extremely limited in its functions and jurisdiction.

In the spirit of the Founders, John C. Calhoun saw that the restrictions on majority rule were not in every respect working as they had been intended. Contrary to Madison's expectation that various interests in a large country would check each other, different interests had concentrated in different regions, making a "numerical majority" that exploited a minority. Some few small additions were therefore needed in the accepted devices by which the majority was to be restrained.

Further, Calhoun illuminated the moral principle behind such restrictions, which he summed up as the "concurrent majority." The "mere numerical majority" was not itself an ethical or an adequately democratic idea. What was needed was a higher consensus, a larger majority reaching a decision after deliberation and compromise—a process that could only be invoked by investing the minority with certain institutionalized powers of self-defense. Far from being a rejection of majority rule, the resulting consensus was democratically and morally preferable to the dictate of a 51 percent majority, which might itself be merely a temporary and expedient coalition of self-seekers. A blue ribbon commission in Britain, which recently delivered the most extensive and hopeful report ever made on the problems of Northern Ireland, makes Calhoun the centerpiece of its proposals.

There is certainly nothing in the least un-American or undemocratic in a philosophical consideration of the imperfections of majority rule, or of the possibility of different constitutional arrangements. The only thing that is really threatened by such discussion is the democratic orthodoxies of those who wish to keep all public debate in channels approved by themselves.

There is an even deeper dishonesty here—because, in fact, there are extant at this moment in American society institutionalized special privileges for blacks that violate majority rule (as well as traditional principles of law), since a clear majority, for instance, disapproves of affirmative action and busing, Race norming in employment, double prosecution of offenses against blacks, reparations rather than punishment for riots, and much else is already institutionalized in our society. Real majority rule is the last thing our present regime wants.

They want something quite different: not a right of defense, but a permanent untouchable privilege under an imperial state—for a guaranteed income levy on the majority. Here lies the real problem and the real abandonment of democracy.

If we are to be true to the American inheritance, society must precede government; the community must take precedence over the state. This simple declaration, I realize, does not grapple fully with the complexities of modern life, with the thrust of the predominant strain of the national character, and with the burdens, including the international role, that history has piled upon us. However, I am talking about philosophical starting points, not final solutions.

If it is indeed true that man is capable of self-government, then it is true that his mistakes are to some degree reversible. Much could be accomplished toward the preservation and reordering of self-government if we could reorder our thinking to give society precedence over government and make our communities the master of the state rather than its raw material.

The concurrent majority is a complex concept and one wonders if many of those who have written about it have understood it in its amplitude. It is not primarily about constitutional devices, nor about the balancing of competing material interests, though both of these things figure in it subsidiarily. It is about, rather, the ethical questions that confront a government resting on the consent of the people. The fundamental question with which Calhoun wrestles in all his works is how to achieve and maintain the proper balance between power and liberty in a democratic society. In the final analysis Calhoun engages in, and invites us to engage in, an exercise of applying realistically to the public business of the American Union what Russell Kirk has called "the moral imagination."

"A Senator of Rome when Rome Survived." The Unknown Calhoun

OF THE GREAT TRIUMVIRATE who dominated American public discourse from the War of 1812 till the mid-19th century, John C. Calhoun was the first to depart the scene, in 1850. Henry Clay and Daniel Webster lived a few more years. In a generous eulogy for the man who had been his opponent for forty years, Webster, realizing that an epoch of American history was drawing to a close, called Calhoun "a Senator of Rome when Rome survived." Calhoun's aspirations were always "high, honorable, and noble," Webster said, and "nothing low or selfish" ever "came near the heart or the head of Mr. Calhoun."

To appreciate Webster's words it is necessary to appreciate the importance which the example of the Roman Republic had for the first generations of independent Americans. The republican heroes of ancient Rome, as known through Livy and other historians, were models of principled republican patriotism in a world that had long been dominated by feudalism and monarchy. A statue of George Washington in a toga was considered very appropriate. Indeed, Washington's favorite literary work was Joseph Addison's play about the Roman hero "Cato." The upper chamber of American legislators were known as Senators, and they met in a capitol building. The model hero for American republicans was Cincinnatus, who left his plow to lead an army in successful defense of his country and then took up the plow again without any thought of using his prestige for personal ambition that might undermine the public liberty. (It doesn't matter that some historians assert that our forefathers did not really understand Rome. The significant point is what their beliefs say about them.)

The notion that Calhoun was all about slavery and nothing but slavery is a product of the current reign of Cultural Marxism and does not represent a balanced view of American history. It has not always been so. In 1950 Margaret Coit's admiring biography, *John C. Calhoun: American Portrait*, won a Pulitzer Prize. In 1959 a committee chaired by John F. Kennedy named Calhoun as one of the five greatest Senators of all time. Calhoun's *A Disquisition on Government* has been recognized in every generation and internationally as among the most important political treatises written by an American.

It is somewhat ridiculous to single out Calhoun as a defender of slavery when no one in his time proposed any serious solution to the slavery question. Indeed, Lincoln himself on his election declared he would not know what to do about slavery even if he had the power, which he did not have. Calhoun was forthright in condemning agitation in the North about slavery in the South, warning that it was threatening the bonds of Union. In the last few years of his life, in response to the Wilmot Proviso, which barred the South from use of the new territories acquired from Mexico in violation of the Missouri Compromise, Calhoun did become the most conspicuous proponent of a defensive Southern unity within the Union. By that time Calhoun already occupied the position of elder statesman who was admired and listened to by thoughtful people North and South for his adherence to principle and independence of political party maneuvers.

He had been an eloquent and tireless leader of the House of Representatives during the War of 1812 and one of the main architects of postwar legislation in which he had shown a constructive spirit generous to the welfare of every part of the Union. As Secretary of War, a thankless post, Calhoun had been one of the ablest department heads ever serving in the U.S. government. He had been elected Vice President virtually without opposition and had resigned from that position on a matter of principle. His years of service in the Senate (1833–1843, 1845–1850) were interrupted by a year as Secretary of State. It is a measure of his stature that when President Tyler nominated him to be Secretary of State, at a time of impending conflict with both Britain and Mexico, Calhoun was confirmed by the Senate in a matter of hours without a single dissenting vote, even from the antislavery Senators of Vermont.

Nor was Calhoun a "cast-iron man"—except in principles. His image today is a good object lesson in the proclivity of some historians to resort to cartoon versions of history when dealing with figures they do not like. The description of the "cast-iron" man so often quoted was made by a cranky Englishwoman who met him once briefly. And the Brady daguerreotype usually displayed to portray Calhoun as a dour fanatic was taken during his final illness. Portraits and commentary offer abundant evidence that Calhoun was a handsome, charming, and approachable, as well as a brilliant man.

Americans have long been predominantly a pragmatic people, eager to get on with what seems desirable public policy without much attention to principles and philosophy. So that much of what the Roman Calhoun regarded as necessary for the preservation of a healthy republic will seem strange and irrelevant, or even repulsively stern in the twenty-first century. On the other hand, his observations often are those of a gifted prophet who accurately foresaw perils that the United States has failed to avoid.

A good example of Calhoun's insistence on republican virtue: In 1842, near the end of the session, the Senate was hearing routine committee reports. A report recommending compensation to the heirs of General William Hull brought Calhoun to his feet:

> Mr. Calhoun said that he was not a little surprised... He was, in the first place, surprised that the representatives of General Hull should ever think of presenting this claim to Congress. He would not be more so, if the representatives of [Benedict] Arnold should present a claim for his pay as a general in our service...on the ground that he held the commission of a general, which had not been revoked... He could never forget the deep and universal indignation which pervaded the whole country on the surrender of Detroit [by Hull at the beginning of the War of 1812, without firing a shot] ... How could his pay as Governor be allowed, when there was, for the time, no such Territory as Michigan? It had, by his own act, become a British province and remained so until it was re-conquered by the army under General Harrison. With what show, then, of justice or equity, could he be paid for governing a territory, that did not

exist, and which had ceased to exist by his own act? The error of the committee consisted in supposing that the commission—the mere paper and wax—and not the service, gave the pay.

A similar recurrence to antique republican honor was evoked when the Smithson bequest came before the Senate. James Smithson, a wealthy Englishman, had willed to the United States an endowment for a university. Calhoun observed that Congress in fulfilling the bequest would be allowing a foreigner to empower it to do what had previously been determined to be unconstitutional. "I not only regard the measure as unconstitutional," he said, "but to me it appears to involve a species of meanness which I cannot describe, a want of dignity wholly unworthy of this Government." He continued, "We would accept a donation from a foreigner to do with it what we have no right to do, and just as if we were not rich enough ourselves to do what is proposed, or too mean to do it if it were in our power."

Calhoun believed that government expenditures should be minimal and closely monitored. It was unusual in his time and is perhaps shocking to Americans who have long since thought of politics mostly as a jockeying for government benefits. "We robbed the people in levying taxes. It was plunder and nothing more... Every cent removed from the hands of Government is so much added to the wealth of the people... Every dollar we can prevent from coming into the treasury, or every dollar thrown back into the hands of the people, will tend to strengthen the cause of liberty, and unnerve the arm of power." This sentiment did not mean that he approved the plans of politicians to "distribute" to the governments of the States a treasury surplus brought about by an unjust tariff. This was not giving it back to the people from whom it had been unnecessarily taken, but merely expanding the opportunity for politicians to buy support. In what must be one of the most extraordinary acts of principle in American history, South Carolina refused its share of the unjust distribution.

On other occasions Calhoun called the attention of the Senate to unwelcome truths: "We all knew that when a public building was commenced that it was never finished under five times the original estimate." It was almost impossible to repeal a tax once it had been placed on the books, he said. And whatever the claims of political parties: "All Administrations were nearly alike extravagant ... It was impossible to force the minds of the public officers to the importance of attendance to the public money because we have too much of it." "I have no doubt, from what I daily see," said the stern republican, "that our whole system is rapidly becoming a mere money making concern to those, who have the control of it; and that every feeling of patriotism is rapidly sinking into an universal spirit of avarice."

A modern authority on banking and currency has written that John C. Calhoun understood that complex and contentious subject better than any public man of his time. Characteristically, he refused to be drawn into the party argument between the Whigs and Democrats over whether there should be a national bank or not. He made a deep historical study and his speeches of the 1830s and 1840s on this subject are models of learning and independent statesmanship. Both parties were failing to deal with the fundamental question—who should control the money supply (currency and credit) of the country? The Democrats' Independent Treasury, to do the government's banking business instead of a national bank or Jackson's corrupt system of "pet banks," was a step in the right direction. However, it did not go far enough. The Independent Treasury would continue the long established government policy of treating the notes of private banks as acceptable money Therefore, the banking system would retain a large amount of control over the money supply (its expansion or contraction) which meant great power over the whole economy and every other interest. "We must curb the banking system," said Calhoun, "or it will certainly ruin the country."

> I do not hesitate to say, if Genl. [Alexander] Hamilton had not issued his circular directing bank-notes to be received as gold & silver in the public dues, and if the Bank of the United States had not been created, the whole course of politics under our system would have been entirely different.

Further, why should the U. S. government, which had a large income, create a national debt by borrowing money from bankers, who thus were paid interest at no risk to themselves? Rather, there should be a complete "divorce" of the government and the bankers. Congress had the responsibility to provide a sound circulating currency for the business of the country. The government should issue its own money, Treasury notes, which, based on its credit, would fulfill this obligation and eliminate the connection with bankers.

When the Independent Treasury came to a vote, Calhoun offered an amendment to phase out the Treasury's receipt of bank-notes. The majority Northern Democrats were not about to offend the bankers and his proposal was voted down. Very seldom has a more fundamental challenge been offered to "business as usual." Calhoun had cut through party polemics to the fundamental truth: the alliance of government and bankers gave control of the money supply to private interests to the detriment of every other interest in society. "'It has been justly stated by a British writer," Calhoun told the Senate, " that the power to make a small piece of paper, not worth one cent, by the inscribing of a few names, to be worth a thousand dollars, was a power too high to be entrusted to the hands of mortal men."

As always, Calhoun's ultimate concern was not with money but with the health of republican liberty. He deplored the effects of the banking system on the public morale. The unnatural rewards of banking were diverting able young men from the honorable and useful learned professions and their attention from patriotic service.

Calhoun's warnings of the degeneration of statesmanship due to the development of party organizations and professional politicians was a great source of appeal to thoughtful people in every part of the Union. The Hamiltonians and Jeffersonians had been patriots who had fought over differing visions of America. But the Whigs and the Democrats were primarily election machines. Their campaigns avoided real issues and sought to occupy the non-controversial middle, to be all things to all men. When the issue was protective tariff or no protective tariff, Andrew Jackson had come out for a "judicious tariff." In 1840 the Whigs elected a president with a noisy and meaningless campaign.

In 1844 when the important issue was the status of Texas, the Whig frontrunner Clay and the Democratic frontrunner Van Buren colluded to not mention the issue at all in the presidential campaign, because a clear stand could make trouble for both. Calhoun as Secretary of State disdained this evasion and forced the issue of Texas into prominence. Van Buren thus lost the nomination to a pro-Texas candidate, James K. Polk.

As Calhoun wrote a young friend:

> The Federal Government is no longer under the control of the people, but of a combination of active politicians, who are banded together under the name of Democrats or Whigs, and whose exclusive object is to obtain the control of the honors and emoluments of the Government. They have the control of the almost entire press of the country, and constitute a vast majority of Congress, and of all the functionaries of the Federal Government. With them, a regard for principle, or this or that line of policy, is a mere pretext. They are perfectly indifferent to either, and their whole effort is to make up on both sides such issues as they may think for the time to be the most popular, regardless of truth or consequences.

Calhoun was a vigorous critic of the solidifying system of political party "conventions of the people" to make platforms and nominate candidates. Such proceedings did not represent the voice of the people, but were gatherings of self-interested politicians held together by patronage or the promise of patronage. And were invariably stage-managed and predetermined by clever professional politicians. "This wholesale traffic in public office for party purposes is wholly pernicious and destructive of popular rights," Calhoun said. The "people individually, have no choice, but to vote for the one ticket or the other ticket ... Never was a scheme better contrived to transfer power from the body of the community, to those whose occupation is to get or hold offices .... "

A 21st century American, contemplating the bottomed-out "approval ratings" of public officials, might be inclined to consider Calhoun as a prophet:

> When it comes to be once understood that politics is a game; that those who are engaged in it but act a part; that they make this or that profession, not from honest conviction, or intent to fulfill it, but as the means of deluding the people, and through that delusion to acquire power; when such professions are to be entirely forgotten, the people will lose all confidence in public men. All will be regarded as mere jugglers—the honest and the patriotic as well as the cunning and the profligate—and the people will become indifferent and passive to the grossest abuses of power, on the ground that those whom they may elevate, under whatever pledges, instead of reforming, will but imitate the example of those whom they have expelled.

On another occasion he remarked that in order for self-government of the people to work:

> It will be by drawing into the Presidential canvass and fully discussing all the great questions of the day. One of my strong objections to the caucus system is that it stifles such discussions, and gives the ascendancy to intrigue & management over reason & principles. It is in fact an admirable contrivance to keep the people ignorant and debased.

It was frequently said by opponents and has been repeated by historians that Calhoun was too idealistic for politics. One superficial historian has even said that Calhoun "was out of touch with reality" during the Nullification crisis of 1831–1833, despite the fact that Calhoun and his "gallant little State," standing against almost the entire political power of the Union, achieved a reduction of the tariff.

Such critics miss the point. Calhoun was not out of touch with reality, he simply disdained the "reality" of ordinary political expediency and compromise. He strove to be a statesman. A politician was one who cut deals to achieve and keep office. The duty of a statesman was to acquaint the people with the big picture, with the long-range consequences of seemingly expedient measures. A statesman would foresee avoidable dangers. Near the end of his life Calhoun solemnly and accurately predicted that unless his countrymen changed their ways, the Union would be disrupted within a decade.

Calhoun strongly supported the War of 1812, which he regarded as a necessary defense of American honour against intolerable provocation. There was much opposition to the war. Calhoun made these sensible and moderate remarks to the House of Representatives on the question of opposition in wartime:

> How far the minority in a state of war may justly oppose the measures of government, is a question of the greatest delicacy. On the one side, an honest man, if he believed the war to be unjust or unwise, would not disavow his opinion; but on the contrary, an upright man would do no act, whatever he might think of the war, to put his country in the power of the enemy. It is this double aspect of the subject which indicates the course that reason approbates. Among ourselves at home we may contend; but whatever is requisite to give the reputation and the arms of the republic superiority over its enemy, it is the duty of all, the minority no less than the majority, to support... In some cases it may possibly be doubtful, even to the most conscientious, how to act. It is one of the misfortunes of differing from the rest of the community on the subject of war.

In monarchies, the decision to go to war was made by the ruler. But for the United States, war "ought never to be resorted to except when it is clearly justifiable and necessary." In a republic, war must never be undertaken except when circumstances "will justify it in the eye of the nation." And war must always be undertaken gravely and honorably, without "bullying" and threats "nor the ardor of eloquence to inflame our passions."

It is in regard to foreign relations and war that Calhoun made his most telling and unheeded prophecies about the consequences of violating true republican principles. Calhoun delighted in the expansion of the American people across the continent. It was the very energy and enterprise of the American people that made war unnecessary. Their own unofficial efforts would bring under American control all the territory that could reasonably be desired:

> Peace is, indeed, our policy. Providence has cast our lot on a portion of the globe sufficiently vast to satisfy the most grasping ambition, and abounding in resources above all others, which only require to be fully developed to make us the greatest and most prosperous people on earth.... Let a durable and firm peace be established, and this Government be confined rigidly to the few great objects for which it was instituted; leaving the States to contend in generous rivalry, to develop, by the arts of peace, their respective resources, and a scene of prosperity and happiness would follow heretofore unequalled on the globe.

The U.S. government had no need for provocative words and acts, much less conflicts with other powers. All the government needed was a policy of "masterly inactivity." As Secretary of State he worked toward a compromise with Great Britain over the Oregon territory, realizing that despite the demands of some for "Fifty-Four Forty or Fight," it would be counterproductive to go to war with the greatest power on earth where there was no possibility to place and supply an army. After much bluster, the Polk administration was forced to accept the compromise settlement that Calhoun had made.

Calhoun's statesmanship never showed better, perhaps, than in his stand on the Mexican War. Texas had won its own independent nationhood, and thanks to John Tyler and Calhoun had become a member of the American Union. Tensions remained high with Mexico over the boundaries of Texas and other matters. Polk on assuming office sent an army force to occupy the barren land between the Nueces and Rio Grande rivers, which Mexicans asserted was not part of Texas. A clash occurred with Mexican forces in the disputed area. When the news of this reached Washington, Polk declared that "American blood has been shed on American soil" and asked Congress to recognize a state of war.

Calhoun raised a lonely voice against the surge of patriotism that ensued. He refused to support the war resolution in the Senate. A border incident did not necessarily call for all-out war, he said. Most importantly, a perilous precedent had been set. The President had in effect initiated a war without waiting for the people or Congress. If this precedent were allowed to stand, it would empower any future President to commit the country to war at will. And so it has been.

We can measure the quality of Calhoun's statesmanship and love of democratic government when we realize that the war was very popular, especially in the South, and when we compare him with most of the Whigs in Congress. Opposed to the war and the Polk administration, they nevertheless voted for the war resolution out of fear of being branded as unpatriotic, and then voted no on all legislation to supply the army.

As the war progressed Calhoun repeatedly argued for limited war aims and against the rising clamor of Manifest Destiny. Let the U.S. be satisfied with Texas, New Mexico, and California and not invade and occupy Mexico. His remarks might apply to the 21st century as well as the 19th:

> We make a great mistake in supposing all people are capable of self-government. Acting under that impression, many are anxious to force free governments on all the people of this continent, and over the world, if they had the power. It has been lately urged in a very respectable quarter, that it is the mission of this country to spread civil and religious liberty over the globe, and

especially over this continent—even by force if necessary. It is a sad delusion. None but a people advanced to a high state of intellectual and moral excellence are capable, in a civilized condition, of forming and maintaining free governments; and among those who are so far advanced, very few indeed have had the good fortune to form constitutions capable of endurance.

The attempt to create a free government in Mexico would only result in the U.S. installing and permanently propping up by force a puppet government, as the British had done in India. Sound familiar?

At this time Calhoun wrote his daughter, his closest confidante:

Our people have undergone a great change. Their inclination is for conquest & empire, regardless of their institutions & liberty; or, rather, they think they hold their liberty by a divine tenure, which no imprudence, or folly on their part can defeat... We act, as if good institutions & liberty belong to us of right, & that neither neglect nor folly can deprive us of their blessing.

To those of a conservative disposition, Calhoun may seem to be a prophet, the full import of whose warnings are yet to be seen.

About the Author

CLYDE WILSON is Emeritus Distinguished Professor of History at the University of South Carolina where he was the editor of the multi-volume *The Papers of John C. Calhoun*. He is the M.E. Bradford Distinguished Chair at the Abbeville Institute. He is the author or editor of over 40 books and over 700 articles, essays, and reviews. Dr. Wilson is co-founder and co-publisher of Shotwell Publishing, a source for unappologetically Southern books.

Latest Releases & Best Sellers

OVER 70 UNAPOLOGETICALLY SOUTHERN
TITLES FOR YOU TO ENJOY

SHOTWELLPUBLISHING.COM

Free Book Offer

DON'T GET LEFT OUT, Y'ALL.
Sign-up and be the first to know about new releases, sales, and other goodies —plus we'll send you TWO FREE EBOOKS!

Lies My Teacher Told Me:
The True History of the War for Southern Independence
by Dr. Clyde N. Wilson

&

Confederaphobia:
An American Epidemic
by Paul C. Graham

FreeLiesBook.com

Southern Books. No Apologies.
We love the South — its history, traditions, and culture — and are proud of our inheritance as Southerners. Our books are a reflection of this love.

www.ingramcontent.com/pod-product-compliance
Lightning Source LLC
Chambersburg PA
CBHW062013180426
43199CB00035B/2638